The Civil War Navy in Florida

The Civil War Navy in Florida

Robert A. Mattson

Published by the Author
2014

The Civil War Navy in Florida

Copyright © 2014 by Robert A. Mattson

All rights reserved. This book or any portion thereof may not be reproduced or used in any manner whatsoever without the express written permission of the publisher except for the use of brief quotations in a book review or scholarly journal.

First Printing: 2014

ISBN 978-0-692-25874-3

Published by the Author
East Palatka, FL 32131

yelpmark@aol.com

Printed in the United States of America by IngramSpark.

Quotations from naval officers' reports, unless otherwise noted, are cited from the "Official Records of the Union and Confederate Navies in the War of the Rebellion," U.S. Government Printing Office.

Front cover illustrations:

BACKGROUND – U.S. Coast Survey 1857 bathymetric map of the mouth of the Apalachicola River (Florida State Archives, Florida Memory Project).

OVERLAY PHOTOS – top, USS *Mercedita*; middle, USS *Montgomery* (both courtesy Naval History and Heritage Command); bottom, Apalachicola waterfront in the late 1800s (Florida State Archives, Florida Memory Project).

Contents

Foreword ix

Chapter 1. The Civil War Navies.. 1
    The Union and Confederate Navies at the Start of the War.... 1
    The Union Blockade and its Officers 6
    Confederate Navy Officers 11
    The Men of the Navies 14
    The U.S. and C.S. Marines in the Civil War............................ 21
    The Confederate Cruisers 22

Chapter 2. The Naval War in Florida and the Start of the Civil War. 24
    General Overview – Florida and the Navies at the Start of the War 24
    Takeover of Coastal Fortifications in Florida........................... 26
    Florida Lighthouses... 29
    Pensacola Navy Yard – 1861 31
    Key West, Headquarters of the East Gulf Blockading Squadron 34
    The Navy War in Florida was a River War.............................. 35
    The Blockade comes to Florida 37
    Union Navy Officers in Florida... 39
    Confederate Navy Officers in Florida...................................... 44

Chapter 3. Actions in the Panhandle 1861-1864.............................. 46
    Pensacola Bay and the Pensacola Navy Yard 46
    St. Andrews Bay and Confederate Salt Works 52
    Apalachicola River and Bay 60
    St. Marks River and Adjacent Waters..................................... 68

Chapter 4. Actions in Northeast Florida 1862-1864 74
    Retaking Ft. Clinch and Occupation of Fernandina 74
    Entering the St. Johns River and First Union Occupation of Jacksonville... 78
    The Union Navy, Union Loyalists, Confederates, and the Slave Population 81
    Actions with Confederate Battery at St. Johns Bluff............... 83
    USN Patrol Activity on the St. Johns River, 1862 90
    USN Patrol Activity on the St. Johns River, 1863 93
    The Confederates Fight Back, 1864 94

Chapter 5. Actions in South Florida 1862-1864.............................. 100
    Mosquito Inlet/New Smyrna 100
    The Southern St. Johns River 106

    The Indian River Lagoon/Southeast Florida 109
    Southwest Florida/Charlotte Harbor 114

Chapter 6. Actions in Tampa Bay and on the Big Bend Coast 1861-1864 121
    Tampa Bay 121
    The Lower Big Bend.. 127
    Cedar Keys/Suwannee River 133
    The Upper Big Bend.. 138

Chapter 7. The War Ends – Actions in 1865 and Concluding Thoughts 144
    Northeast Florida 144
    The Panhandle... 145
    South Florida... 150
    West Florida.. 155
    The Role of the Navy in Florida... 157
    Final Thoughts on the Navy in the Civil War in Florida 160

Appendix 1. Warships of the Florida Blockade............................ 163

Appendix 2. Places to visit and events to attend that cover the Civil War Navies in Florida 173

Bibliography... 183

Index 189

Foreword

My family appears to have a long seafaring tradition, and that seems to have been genetically imprinted on me throughout my life. My Dad served a hitch in the U.S. Navy during the Korean War, and most of my best friends and colleagues were U.S. Navy sailors. My Granddad on my father's side served in one of the Scandinavian Navies and Merchant Marine service, and it appears that Mattson's going back into history were seafaring people.

I was first introduced to the hobby of Civil War "re-enacting," or perhaps more accurately "Civil War living history interpretation" by a friend of my wife's. When we lived in Lake City, Florida, he would come by to visit us every year on his way to participate in the Olustee Battle re-enactment outside of Lake City each February; a re-creation of the largest Civil War battle fought in Florida. Eventually, I met up with the USS *Fort Henry* Living History Association, a living history group who specialize in interpretation of U.S. Navy and Marine personnel during the Civil War.

These combinations of experiences got me interested in doing Civil War living history interpretation of the naval side of the war, because most folks don't even think of the navies when they think of the Civil War. The massive land combat between the armies of that period naturally draws an immense amount of attention, yet the navies (both North and South) were a key component of the conflict and contributed immensely to its outcome, one way or another. Ever since I have started in the hobby, the standard question from spectators when I am doing a U.S. Navy sailor at events is,"Navy!! What's the Navy doing here?" "Ah, yes, let me tell you," I answer, and proceed from there.

For the past four years, I have been a Guest Blogger with the "Civil War Navy Sesquicentennial" Blog, an official web site sponsored by the Naval History and Heritage Command (a branch of the Unites States Navy). The purpose of this site is to celebrate, call attention to, and provide information on the activities of the Union and Confederate Navies on the 150th Anniversary of the Civil War, which is going on right now (2011-2015). During this experience, I have accumulated an immense quantity of notes, illustrations, and background material on the activities of the navies in Florida that made me wonder if I could put together an entire book on the Civil War naval experience in Florida, especially during this Sesquicentennial of the War. This volume is the result of that, and I sincerely thank the folks at IngramSpark/Lightning Source Printing for helping me publish this for you to read.

I have relied heavily on the works of others to stitch together this account. These are in the Bibliography at the end of the book. My main source of information, however, was the massive collection known as the "Official Records of the Union and Confederate Navies in the War of the Rebellion," published by the U.S. Navy after the war. This 30-volume collection compiles all of the written orders, dispatches, after-action reports and official correspondence of Union and Confederate naval officers during the war. I have quoted liberally from the officers' reports from this source, as I hope that it adds an immediacy, a "you are there" sort of feeling, to my narrative. Where I could, I included quotes from the letters or diaries of junior officers and men on Navy ships. It was not my intent to produce a scholarly treatise, because I was unable to go to the Library of Congress, the Naval History and Heritage Command, etc. to access primary sources such as ship's deck logs, personal papers of naval officers, and similar material. My intent was to produce something readable that is solidly grounded in the historical scholarship available to me and that would give the interested reader a thorough feel for the hard work done by the sailors and marines who served in Florida and the perils they faced during the war.

I would like to acknowledge many folks who helped me (whether they knew it or not) with putting this book together. First, my "shipmates" with the USS *Fort Henry* Living History Association have been invaluable. Marine Sgt. Dave Ekardt was particularly helpful in pointing me to actions and events to include in the book. I also appreciate my buddies at the Hampton Roads Naval Museum in Norfolk, VA, who gave me a chance to explore my interest in Civil War naval history in Florida and blog about it on the "CWN150" blog site, and also provided lots of valuable background information; these are Matt (now with the Naval Historical Foundation), Gordon, and Laura. After all those "thanks," any errors, inaccuracies or omissions in this account are solely my fault.

I am so very grateful to the artists and photographers who have allowed me to use their work in this book. Renowned Florida history artist Jackson Walker contributed an image of one of his paintings from the "Legendary Florida" collection for use in Chapter 5. Karen Lou Rogers and Tiffany Trent contributed their photographs. Dr. Keith Holland allowed me to use an illustration of the Union steamer *Maple Leaf* from his work to document the salvage of that ship. Lastly, but in no way least, Kevin Mouyard worked very hard to put together a series of superb maps depicting the areas of Florida I cover and the naval actions there. Darlene Swanson did the final formatting on the book's cover for me.

I also need to thank some fellow authors who have been so very helpful. Jack Owen, local author in Palatka of several books, has offered much valuable advice, ideas and counsel. Nancy Quatrano provided copy editing on some of this manuscript, and also many helpful ideas and suggestions. I thank both of them for their encouragement. Kristin at Read/Think Books in Palatka has also been a source of inspiration.

And lastly it may seem trite, but it is genuine; my wife, Karen, has been a constant companion on this journey. It seems over the past few years most of our get-aways together alone have been associated with a CW Navy living history or re-enactment event. She has wondered,"When are we going to go away and NOT do something Civil War Navy?" I promise that we will do that.

This book is dedicated to my Dad, who passed away as I was putting it together; may he now rest always in that never-ending "safe harbor."

Rob Mattson

Chapter 1. The Civil War Navies

The Union and Confederate Navies at the Start of the War

When war broke out between the northern states and those of the south that seceded, the U.S. Navy had a grand total of 76 ships (some accounts say 90 ships), of which 42 were actually commissioned and in service (the remaining ships were "laid up in ordinary" or moth-balled as we say today). Of these 42 warships, 30 were on foreign stations at the war's beginning. Initially, but four ships were available in northern ports to implement the blockade of the southern coastline, declared by newly-elected President Abraham Lincoln in April 1861.

Secretary of the U.S. Navy Gideon Welles. Naval History and Heritage Command.

Lincoln appointed New England native Gideon Welles to the post of Secretary of the U.S. Navy, who began his office on March 7, 1861. Welles' naval experience was limited to a stint as the head of the USN's Bureau of Provisions and Clothing from 1846-1849. Imbued with a strong work ethic, Welles compensated for his lack of naval knowledge first, by virtue of his talents as an able administrator who could see the "big picture" policy issues, and second, by appointing former naval officer Gustavus Vasa Fox as his assistant.

Fox was appointed chief clerk in May 1861, and eventually Welles created the position of Assistant Secretary of the Navy for him. Fox handled all of the technical and bureaucratic details of administering the Navy (with which he was very familiar), leaving Welles free to set policy and coordinate with the President. Welles also created various advisory boards to help chart naval strategy for the war effort. They included the Commission on Conference, also known as the Blockade Board, and the Ironclad Board. These committees drafted detailed briefing papers laying out strategy options and recommendations for Welles and the President to consider.

Merchant steamers *E.B. Hale* and *Stars and Stripes* being converted into U.S. Navy gunboats. Both saw service in the Florida blockade. Naval History and Heritage Command.

To expand the U.S. Navy, Welles initiated a dual program of new warship construction and the purchase of existing vessels which were reconfigured into gunboats. An assortment of schooners, barks, merchant steamers, ferryboats, and other vessels became U.S. Navy gunboats. Initially he dispatched naval officers to evaluate and make purchases, but it soon became evident that they were being swindled by unscrupulous profiteers who were selling them questionable vessels at highly inflated prices. Welles turned to his brother-in-law, George D. Morgan, to deal with purchasing ships in New York, and his friend John Murray Forbes to handle purchases in Boston. Both were shrewd, tough businessmen who could deal with the "wheeler-dealers" in the two harbors. Welles was accused of nepotism, for hiring a relative, and criticized for giving them a free hand in matters of purchase and for allowing them to draw a commission from their purchases, but both men secured a large number of ships for the U.S. Navy at cut-rate prices. By the end of the war, the U.S. Navy was the second largest in the world at 671 commissioned warships. Over 51,000 sailors manned these ships.

The Civil War was the period of transition from sailing to steam-powered navies. A number of ships in both navies were pure steamships, driven by paddle wheels, or by a "screw", a propeller on a shaft protruding from the stern of the ship. Most of the larger ships (Union Navy frigates and sloops and Confederate Navy high-seas commerce raiders) were powered by both a sail rig and a steam engine. The antiquated biases of many of the senior officers in the U.S. Navy refused to accept the transition to a steam navy, as they were "raised in a sailing navy," and they thought that it should always be that way. This hampered the evolution of the U.S. Navy after the Civil War.

In contrast to the Union, there did not exist a Confederate Navy at the war's beginning. Confederate States of America President Jefferson Davis appointed Stephen R. Mallory as Secretary of the Confederate Navy on March 4, 1861. Born circa 1812-13 in Trinidad, he was raised mostly in Key West, Florida. He began his professional career in the early 1800s practicing maritime law in the Florida Keys (at the time a hot bed of "wrecking," the recovery of cargo from ships wrecked on the reefs of the Keys). Eventually he went into politics, representing Florida in the U.S. Senate. There, he was appointed to the Senate Committee on Naval Affairs, which he eventually chaired.

During his tenure in this position, he was an advocate for the reinstatement of flogging as a means of discipline of sailors. He failed to prevail on this issue, but he was successful in passing legislation overhauling the means of promotion and retention of officers in the Navy, establishing a Board of Review, which evaluated naval officers based on accomplishments and abandoned the ancient system of advancement based on seniority alone. The other major issue Mallory promoted in his senate position was for the U.S. Navy to adopt emerging technologies, such as construction of ironclad, steam-powered warships.

When Florida seceded, Mallory joined the fledgling Confederacy. He was very well aware that the south could never match the north in the ability to build and modify ships, and that he would never be able to go ship-for-ship against the U.S. Navy; so he adopted a naval strategy based on three things (not in order of priority):

1. Deploy sea-going commerce raiders to disrupt Union merchant shipping and divert Union warships from the blockade to chase the raiders.

2. Run the Union blockade using a combination of private shipping and specially-constructed blockade-running ships operated by the C.S. Navy.

3. Adopt and deploy the broad range of emerging naval technologies (ironclads, submersibles, and torpedoes) to attempt to keep southern harbors open and maintain the flow of supplies through the blockade.

Secretary of the Confederate Navy Stephen R. Mallory. State Archives of Florida, Florida Memory Project.

One could say that he both succeeded and failed in all three. Originally, the Confederate States of America tried to implement commerce raiding by the old device of issuing "Letters of Marque" to allow private parties to act as raiders on behalf of the Confederate government. Due to international treaty barring the practice of privateering, the Confederate Navy eventually decided to assume the responsibility for purchasing and constructing sea-going ships to prey on Union commerce shipping. These would be regular, commissioned warships in the C.S. Navy. While some of these had great success (notably the CSS *Alabama* and *Shenandoah*), they failed to even partially disable Union maritime commerce, although they did contribute to the eventual demise of the U.S. merchant marine industry due to astronomical inflation of insurance costs. They were unsuccessful at diverting Union Navy ships off the blockade to try to hunt them down and capture them.

Blockade running was also initially entrusted to private parties, but the private runners ultimately failed to deliver the war material needed by the Confederacy to prosecute the war. The demand for luxury goods (and the willingness of the Confederate aristocracy to pay whatever price was commanded) made it more lucrative for private runners to carry cargo to meet this demand, despite government requirements that they carry a certain percentage of military cargo. Eventually, the Confederate Navy chose to construct and crew some of its own blockade runners in order to supply arms and equipment to the armies of the Confederacy. These were shallow draft, very fast side-wheel steamers, mostly constructed in Great Britain. They were painted gray or black as camouflage and had low profiles to avoid easy observation.

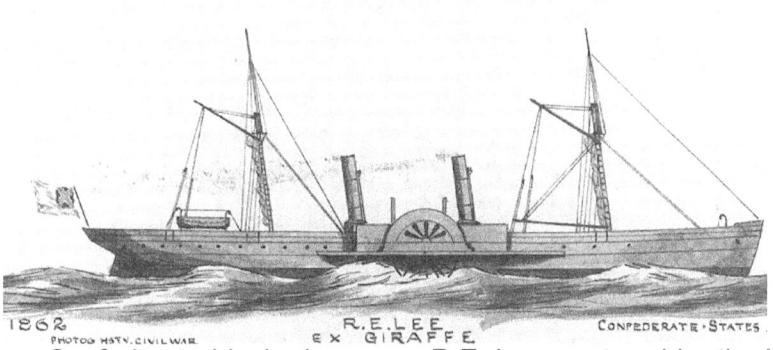

Former Confederate blockade runner *R.E. Lee*, captured by the U.S. Navy and renamed USS *Ft. Donelson*. Erik Heyl sketch from Naval History and Heritage Command.

Mallory's willingness to use technology was perhaps his greatest contribution to the war effort, but again, he was unable to capitalize on this. He embraced the use of ironclad ships as a means of going up against the overwhelming firepower of the big frigates and sloops of the Union Navy, but he did not exercise the necessary degree of authority in prioritizing the construction of the C.S. Navy ironclads. The various private groups contracted to build the ironclads had to compete with one another in the procurement of critically needed iron plates, machinery, skilled personnel, and the other limited resources that the Confederacy had to constantly deal with. This resulted in the construction of mostly ineffective ironclad vessels that failed to live up to their potential. If Mallory had used his authority (and strategic vision) to prioritize which ships needed to be finished first, and divert all resources to those, the Confederate ironclads may have been more effective. The use of submersible vessels (the "*Davids*" and the CSS *Hunley*) did not achieve widespread success, and the use of torpedoes, while extremely effective in the latter stages of the war (in terms of both real results and their psychological impact) were deployed too late to accomplish anything substantive.

The Union Blockade and its Officers

Following President Lincoln's declaration of a blockade of the southern coast on April 19, 1861, the U.S. Navy moved to implement the President's directive. The blockade was initially organized as the Atlantic Blockading Squadron (Flag Officer Silas H. Stringham commanding) and the Gulf Blockading Squadron (Flag Officer William Mervine commanding). Navy warships on foreign stations were recalled, and as they arrived and were refitted, began to take up station on the blockade. The USS *Niagara* took up station off Charleston, SC on May 10, 1861; about two weeks later, the USS *Brooklyn* was off the Mississippi River mouth on May 26 (after helping reinforce the garrison at Ft. Pickens). By early July, Stringham had 22 warships at his disposal, and Mervine had 21.

The overall blockade strategy was set by the Blockade Board, under the leadership of Capt. Samuel F. Du Pont. The Board realized that the extensiveness of the coastline of the Confederacy was both blessing and curse. On the one hand, that extensiveness would make effective implementation of the blockade an immense task; at the same time, it would also make it difficult for the Confederacy to defend. The southern coastline was 3,500 miles in length, stretching from northeastern Virginia to the Texas/Mexico border. Additionally, the Mississippi River added an additional 3,600 miles of shoreline. The Blockade Board conceived of a series of amphibious operations off the Confederate Atlantic and Gulf Coasts to secure bases of operation from which the ships of the Blockade could operate.

Stringham led a squadron of six warships, two army transports and supporting vessels against Hatteras Inlet, NC in August 1861. The result of this expedition was the first of many successful joint U.S. Navy/Army victories along the Confederate coast. Despite this, criticism of Stringham forced his resignation; and the Atlantic Squadron was divided into the North Atlantic Blockading Squadron, under the command of Flag Officer Louis M. Goldsborough, and the South

Atlantic Blockading Squadron. The North Atlantic Squadron was responsible for the coasts of Virginia and N. Carolina, while the South Atlantic Squadron patrolled the coasts of S. Carolina, Georgia, and northeast Florida down to Mosquito Inlet (present-day Ponce de Leon Inlet).

Preparing to fire a warning shot on a blockade runner. From Harper's Weekly, State Archives of Florida, Florida Memory Project.

Initial command of the South Atlantic Blockading Squadron went to Flag Officer Samuel F. Du Pont, who had chaired the Blockade Board. Du Pont had served in the U.S. Navy since 1815, joining as a Midshipman. He was an advocate for reform in the Navy, supporting efforts to streamline and strengthen the system for promoting deserving officers. In July 1862 he was appointed one of the first Rear Admirals in the history of the Navy. Du Pont was succeeded in 1863 by Rear Admiral John A. Dahlgren, who had spent much of the war as a Captain and head of the Bureau of Naval Ordinance. Dalhlgren designed most of the large weaponry used by the U.S. Navy, including the "Dahlgren guns" with their characteristic soda-bottle shape, which comprised the main deck battery of many U.S. Navy ships. These were typically designated with a Roman numeral (e.g., XI (11)-inch gun, IX (9)-inch gun). He also designed a series of excellent boat howitzers, of which nearly every navy ship carried one or more.

Steam frigate USS *Wabash*, flagship of the South Atlantic Blockading Squadron. Naval History and Heritage Command.

Flag Officer (later Rear Admiral) Samuel F. Du Pont, first commanding officer of the South Atlantic Blockading Squadron. Florida Center for Instructional Technology, University of South Florida, used by permission.

Rear Admiral John A. Dahlgren, standing beside one of the Dahlgren guns that he designed. Library of Congress, Prints & Photographs Division, Civil War Photographs, LC-B811-3417

By the beginning of 1862, the Gulf Squadron was similarly divided; into the East Gulf Blockading Squadron, responsible for the Florida Coast from Mosquito Inlet around to St. Andrews Bay, and the West Gulf Blockading Squadron, which had the remainder of the Gulf Coast from St. Andrews Bay to the US/Mexico Border. Additionally, there was a separate Mississippi Squadron, responsible for working with the West Gulf Squadron to take control of the Mississippi River. This arrangement remained throughout the rest of the war.

Initial command of the East Gulf Squadron went to Flag Officer William McKean. McKean was succeeded by Rear Admiral J.L. Lardner, both of whom had a relatively short tenure in their commands due to age and health issues. Command of the East Gulf Squadron then went to Rear Admiral Theodorus Bailey, who remained in this post through most of the remainder of the war. Bailey joined the Navy in January 1818. He served with Farragut in the West Gulf Squadron for the early part of the war and participated in the Union occupation of New Orleans in April 1862. Command of the West Gulf Blockading Squadron went to Flag Officer David G. Farragut, who commanded this squadron for most of the war. A navy veteran of fifty one years of service, some were skeptical that the sixty+ year old Farragut was up to the job when he was appointed, plus there were suspicions as he

Rear Admiral David G. Farragut. Library of Congress, Prints & Photographs Division, Civil War Photographs, LC-B813-1561-A.

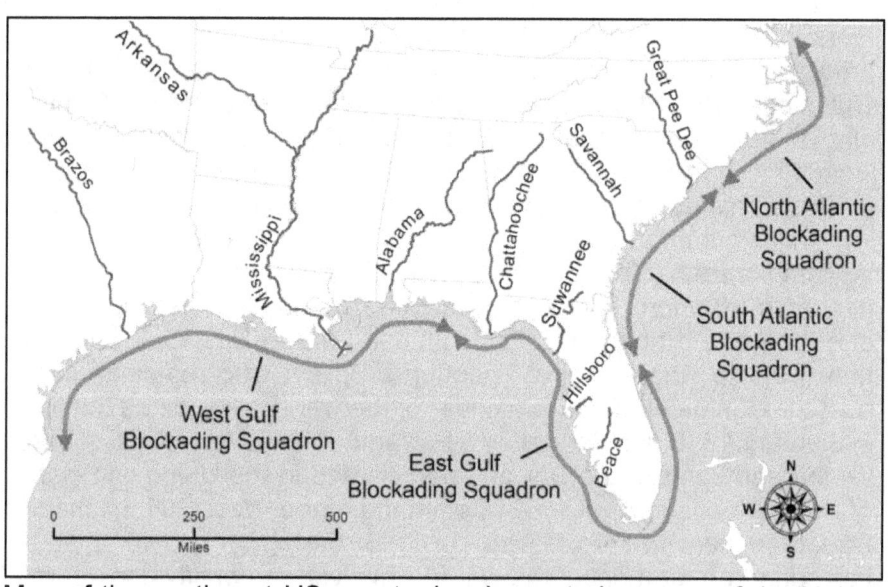

Map of the southeast US coast, showing patrol sectors of the Union Blockading Squadrons.

was a native southerner, born in Tennessee. But he performed brilliantly, becoming one of the most renowned officers in the history of the U.S. Navy. He was promoted as the Navy's first Vice Admiral in 1864; the rank was created for him on the orders of President Lincoln in recognition of his service to the Navy and country. Historian Bruce McPherson believes that Farragut, based on his achievements at New Orleans, on the Mississippi River and at Mobile Bay, ranks with Union Generals Ulysses S. Grant and William Tecumseh Sherman as the three men who essentially won the war for the Union.

Confederate Navy Officers

While southern-born U.S. Navy officers such as Du Pont and Farragut remained loyal to the Union, 259 USN officers resigned their commissions, or were discharged, when the war broke out to join their southern home states (other sources place the total at 373). One of the most senior of these was Capt. Franklin Buchanan. A vet-

Admiral Franklin Buchanan of the Confederate States Navy. Library of Congress, Prints & Photographs Division, Civil War Photographs, LC-B813-1428-A.

eran of forty five years of service in the U.S. Navy, he had an exceptionally distinguished service record. He was the first Commandant of the U.S. Naval Academy, he served as Commodore Matthew Perry's Executive Officer on the historic voyage to Japan, and he commanded the Washington Navy Yard at the outbreak of the war. Convinced that his home state of Maryland would eventually secede, he personally tendered his resignation to Sec. Welles. After it became apparent that Maryland would not secede, Buchanan reconsidered and requested to be reinstated. By now Welles was enraged by the rash of resignations from the Navy, which he considered to be treasonous disloyalty. He decidedly rejected Buchanan's request. Buchanan went on to serve as the highest-ranking officer in the Confederate Navy, its first Admiral. He commanded the ironclad CSS *Virginia* in the historic engagement with the ships of the North Atlantic Blockading Squadron on March 8, 1862. Later in the war, he was the senior officer in command of C.S. Navy forces defending Mobile Bay and he commanded the ironclad CSS *Tennessee* in the battle with Farragut's squadron at the Battle of Mobile Bay in August 1864.

Raphael Semmes (thirty five years of service in the U.S. Navy) resigned his commission in 1861 to join his home state of Alabama. After the firing on Ft. Sumter, he oversaw the conversion of a merchant steamer into the CSS *Sumter*, the first of the Confederate Navy raiders. Semmes was a brilliant seaman, and during the roughly six-month cruise of the *Sumter*, he and his crew captured and/or destroyed eighteen Union prizes. After a short hiatus, Semmes then took command of the CSS *Alabama* in August 1862. The *Alabama* was an ocean-going raider powered by steam and sail. She was built in Liverpool England under secret contract to the Confederacy by the shipping firm John Laird Sons and Company. The Confederates and the English slipped her out of England under the ruse that she was a merchant ship on a shake-down cruise. At sea, she rendezvoused with supply ships that had the ship's heavy guns, small arms and accoutrements, which were transferred aboard. Overall, *Alabama* captured and/or destroyed over 60 Union merchant ships, and even sank the Union Navy gunboat USS *Hatteras* near Galveston Texas in January 1863. The CSN raider was sunk in a single-ship combat engagement with the USS *Kearsarge* off Cherbourg France in June 1864. Semmes was rescued by the English yacht *Deerhound*, returned to the Confederacy, and was promoted as the C.S. Navy's second Admiral (after Buchanan) in command of the CSN James River Squadron.

A famous photo of Capt. Raphael Semmes on the deck of the Confederate raider CSS *Alabama*. His Executive Officer Lt. John M. Kell is in the background next to the ship's helm. Naval History and Heritage Command.

    Josiah Tattnall was a native of Georgia, who resigned his commission with the U.S. Navy to command the Georgia State Navy. He was also one of the most senior officers in the USN, serving for almost fifty years. He had fought for the Navy in the War of 1812, in the Algerine War, chased pirates in the Caribbean, and fought in the Mexican War, during which he was wounded. When the C.S. Navy absorbed the individual state navies, he was placed in command of the naval defenses of South Carolina and Georgia. He engaged U.S. Navy gunboats with his small fleet on the Savannah River during the preparations for the Union siege of Ft. Pulaski, and his rag-tag "Mosquito Fleet" attempted to take on the gunboats of Du Pont's massive armada during the taking of Port Royal, South Carolina. He was given command of the CSS *Virginia* after her engagement with the USS *Monitor* and oversaw the ironclad's destruction a couple months later.

The Men of the Navies

At the beginning of the war, there were six commissioned ranks in the U.S. Navy: Midshipman, Master, Lieutenant, Commander, Captain, and Commodore or Flag Officer. The latter was actually more of an honorific title conferred on a Captain in charge of a squadron of ships. The rank of Admiral did not exist in the U.S. Navy at the beginning of the war. Promotion was based on seniority, which led to a moribund, calcified officer corps with very aged senior officers occupying their positions for many years and many young officers languishing as Lieutenants for much of their career, although a Lieutenant with enough seniority to be in command of a warship might be called by the title "Lieutenant-Commanding." By the latter half of 1862, in an effort to reward initiative and create additional promotional opportunities, the Navy created the ranks of Ensign, Lieutenant Commander, and Rear Admiral. The rank of Commodore was also made an official commissioned rank. The rank of Vice Admiral was created towards the end of the war, in 1864.

Additionally, to provide command officers for the burgeoning USN fleet, the Navy created the position of "Volunteer Officer," which went to those with prior command experience on civilian ships after a short training course on naval etiquette, protocol and command. By the war's end, a majority of the officers serving on USN ships were volunteer officers (with the title "Acting" or "Acting Volunteer" in front of their Navy rank), most of whom returned to civilian life after the war ended. In both Navies, there were also line or "sea" officers, qualified to serve in a command position on a warship, and staff officers, which included those in the Engineering, Medical, Paymaster, and Chaplain Divisions, who were not permitted to have command positions on ships.

As noted earlier, most Confederate Navy officers were former U.S. Navy men who resigned their commissions to join their home southern states in the war effort. The C.S. Navy ended up with many more officers than they had ships for them to command (or seamen to crew them). Many of these officers ended up in the C.S. Army or in charge of coastal defenses. Although 43% of the USN officer corps before the war were men from the south, not all of these resigned; and many remained in the U.S. Navy and loyal to the Union. The rank structure in the Confederate Navy was initially similar to that in the Union Navy (six commissioned ranks), although the rank of Commodore was never made an official rank in the Confederate Navy. By the war's end, the Confederate Navy had the ranks of

Midshipman, Master, Second Lieutenant, First Lieutenant, Commander, Captain, Commodore, and Rear Admiral.

The average Union Navy enlisted man was more likely to hail from a city rather than the countryside. He was older than a typical soldier, averaging 26 years in age, and was most likely from an eastern seaboard state. He was generally more cynical and pessimistic about the war and did not enlist out of a spirit of patriotism. With no sea experience, in 1864 a new recruit was mustered into the service with the rank of Landsman, at a rate of pay of $14/month. After typically two years of sea experience and training, he could expect to be promoted to the rank of Ordinary Seaman, at a pay of $16/month. Acquisition of additional sea experience and more specialized skills resulted in promotion to Seaman at a pay of $20/month. Engineer ratings earned a bit better pay, with a Coal Heaver being paid $20/month and a First-class Fireman $30/month. Towards the end of the war, sailors serving on ironclad warships were paid 25% more than seamen on conventional wooden warships.

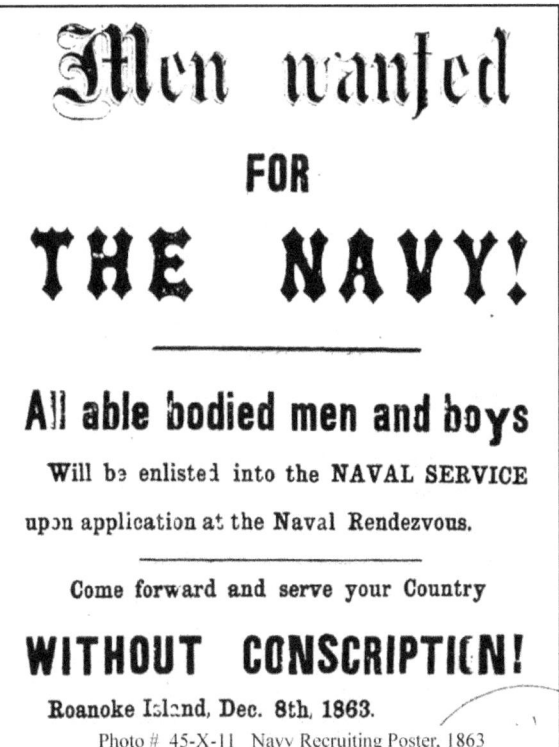

1863 U.S. Navy recruiting poster. Naval History and Heritage Command.

A fully-trained seaman was a highly skilled individual. If the ship had sails, he was knowledgeable and proficient with all of the ship's running rigging (the lines used to raise, lower and trim sails) and with knot-tying and splicing rope. He could serve competently on a crew rowing one of the ship's boats, or could serve as the coxswain ("coxun") steering the boat. On watch, he knew the "points of the compass" and could accurately call out the bearing of a sighted ship from a lookout post in the tops to the deck officer. He could recognize what a ship was by its configuration or silhouette (a schooner, a brig, a steamer, etc.). He was proficient with the use of the ship's small arms complement (pistol, musket, and cutlass), and could serve on a crew manning one of the ship's big guns. The saying was that a good seaman could "hand, reef, and steer." U.S. Navy officers were, for this legitimate reason, always careful on committing their sailors to shore party operations where they might be severely injured or killed.

Non-commissioned navy officers were the Petty Officers, which included the Boatswain ("Bosun") and his mates, responsible for the running of the deck, the Gunner and his mates, responsible for the ship's armament, and the Quartermaster and mates, responsible for manning the ship's helm. The Carpenter and his mates, were responsible for the repair and upkeep of the woodwork of the ship and for damage control during combat. Other Petty Officer ratings included Master at Arms, Ships Steward, Cook, Quarter Gunner, Armorer, Cooper, Captain of the Tops, Captain of the Forecastle, Captain of the Hold, and Captain of the Afterguard. Starting pay for a Petty Officer was $22/month in 1864, although some ratings were paid at a higher rate. Carpenter's Mate pay started at $30/month. Petty officers were also expected to be leaders in shore party combat raids on rebel shore works, along with Marine non-commissioned officers, Sergeants and Corporals.

A Union sailor's pay in the Civil War could be supplemented by prize money. Unfortunately, this was not available to Confederate Navy sailors, as the blockade early on closed the ports where they could send their prizes. The practice of taking prizes dated back at least a century or more in naval services throughout the world. In wartime, a naval ship that captured an enemy ship essentially took possession of that ship. The capturing ship then sent the captor to a port with a USN prize court, which assessed a value to the ship and basically "bought" the ship from the capturing vessel. The prize money was distributed by a formula: half went into a fund to provide income to sailors disabled during their service. Of the remaining half, a percentage went to the Admiral commanding the squadron (many accumulated quite a bit of wealth this way, if they had an aggressive and successful squadron), much of the remaining value of the prize went to the Captain of the capturing ship and its officers, the remainder was distributed among the crew. A Union seaman could supplement his pay by at least a few dollars a month if his ship was successful at capturing prizes. For him, this was financially significant. Some USN recruiting posters emphasized (or over-emphasized) the value of the prizes potentially available at sea as an enticement; one recruiting poster proclaimed "$50,000,000 Prizes!" were already captured as of 1863.

The Union Navy in the Civil War was an integrated Navy. About 16% of the USN enlisted manpower during the war were African Americans, many freed or escaped slaves. Although the degree of egalitarianism probably varied from ship to ship, depending upon the whims and biases of the commander, the preponderance of volunteer officers in command positions on USN warships helped the cause of black sailors, as many of the these officers had commanded them aboard merchant ships and knew their excellent abilities as seamen. As in the Army, African Americans were prohibited from holding a commissioned rank, but they could be given a petty officer rating, and many were. Eight African American U.S. Navy sailors were awarded the Medal of Honor (now known as the "Congressional Medal of Honor") during the war.

A number of seamen in both navies were foreign-born, with a larger proportion of foreigners in the Confederate Navy. In part this was due to the lack of a seafaring tradition in the south, including merchant service, whaling, etc., so few southerners were trained seamen. In part this was also due to most of the larger Confederate warships being built in foreign ports, which provided the sources for crewmen. Some of the Confederate raiders were staffed almost wholly by foreigners except for the officers of the ship, who were native southerners. A few free blacks were known to serve in the Confederate Navy, but the participation of African Americans in that service was restricted to no more than 5% of a particular ship's complement, which limited the participation of African Americans in that navy.

Sailors aboard ship were organized into smaller groups, called "messes"; consisting of 10-15 men, but sometimes being as few as eight. Each mess received a box with cooking and eating ware (pots, plates, etc.). Personal eating/drinking utensils (fork, knife, spoon, and cup) were usually given to a sailor as part of his basic uniform issue, but these would go into the "mess kit". At mealtimes, a representative from the mess would receive the daily ration for each man from the paymaster and would bring this to the cook for preparation, serving as an assistant to the cook in preparing the meal. The mess would

Photo # NH 59430 USS Hunchback's crew

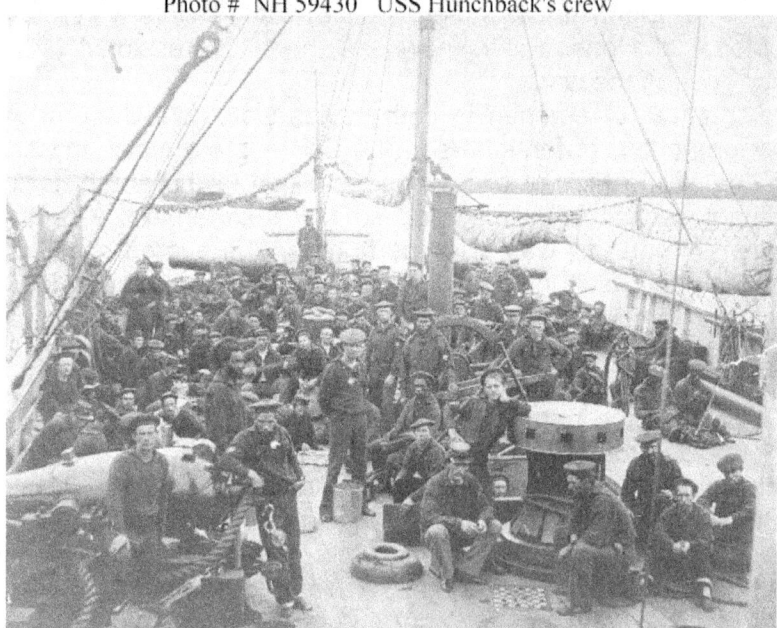

Photo # NH 60873 Crewmembers of USS Miami

(Top) USS *Hunchback* and its crew. Note African American sailors in a group in right background. (Bottom) USS *Miami* and its crew. Note black crewmembers scattered throughout the deck scene. Naval History and Heritage Command.

eat together and generally constituted a sailor's shipboard "family." A typical Union sailor tended to eat better than a typical soldier. This was because it was easier to transport supplies by water, versus wagon or train on land, because of Sec. Welles' commitment to taking good care of "his jack tars" (the sailors referred to him as "Uncle Gideon" because of his concern for their well-being), and because most ships had a staff cook on board, who had received at least some training, or possessed some abilities, in this role. The Army did not have an official position of "cook"; a soldier was typically tapped, willingly or unwillingly, to fulfill this role for a particular army unit.

At the beginning of the war, the U.S. Navy issued a grog ration to sailors aboard USN warships. "Grog" was a mixture of whisky and water (the U.S. Navy declined to use rum because it was "too British," plus whisky was cheaper than rum). Grog was distributed to the crew before breakfast and supper, known in sailor parlance as "splicing the main brace." Grog was issued as a morale booster and be-

Photo # NH 61926   Scene on board USS Pawnee, looking forward

Deck scene on USS *Pawnee*. Note sailor on the bridge with telescope and in the left foreground the running rigging "flemished down" on the deck for appearance. Naval History and Heritage Command.

cause it was believed to help motivate the sailors to undertake some of the less desirable work such as holystoning the deck and coaling the ship. Due in part to many sailors' abuse of alcohol, and under pressure from the temperance movement, to which a number of senior Navy officers were sympathetic (especially Adm. Andrew H. Foote, an ardent "tee-totaler"), the U.S. Congress passed "An Act for the Better Government of the Navy of the United States" in July 1862. Also known as the Reform Act, it abolished the grog ration, which officially went into effect September 1, 1862. In an effort to placate the widespread discontent this move caused, the Navy supplemented the sailors' pay with a bonus of five cents a day (about $1.50/month) after the grog ration was abolished.

A sailor's day was organized in four-hour blocks of time known as "watches." From 8 AM to Noon was the forenoon watch, Noon to 4 PM was the afternoon watch. Two short watches, the first and second dog watch (4-6 PM and 6-8 PM) allowed all hands to have supper, usually the best meal of the day. The first night watch was from 8 PM to Midnight, the middle watch from Midnight to 4 AM, and the morning watch from 4 to 8 AM. Time was kept by the ringing of the ship's bell every half hour. Eight bells sounded at the change of the watch (the end of one and beginning of another). After the first half hour one bell would sound (e.g., one bell in the forenoon watch

Sailors at cutlass drill using "single sticks." Sketch by Alfred R. Waud, Library of Congress, Prints & Photographs Division, Civil War Photographs, DRWG/US – Waud, no. 522 recto (A size).

would be 8:30 AM), then two bells (9 AM), three bells (9:30 AM), etc. When a sailor wasn't "on watch," that is, helping to keep the ship maintained and participating in its operation, or sleeping, he would be engaged in some form of drill. There was general quarters (battle stations) drill, fire drill, drill on the ship's guns, small arms drill, and cutlass drill (using single sticks). When not drilling, he may be part of an instructional class, run by a Senior Petty Officer teaching an advanced skill, such as knot-tying or splicing rope.

The U.S. and C.S. Marines in the Civil War

The U.S. Marines were in existence since the American Revolutionary War, and were a part of the U.S. Navy. For much of the early history of the USN, the traditional role of the Marines mirrored that in the British Royal Navy: to primarily assist in defense of the ship, and to provide security for the officers aboard ship and suppress mutiny. By the Civil War, the Marines were beginning to transition into an expeditionary force that could be used to project power ashore from seaborne forces, although some senior marine officers continued to believe that this was primarily a role for the U.S. Army, and that the role of the Marines should continue to be shipboard defense and discipline. Despite this, Marine detachments on board U.S. Navy blockading ships contributed immensely to the success of shore party raids during the war, as well as other combat operations.

During the course of the war, the total strength of the U.S. Marines never exceeded about 3,800 officers and men throughout the fleet. Their primary responsibilities included shipboard security, helping to maintain shipboard order and discipline, and helping defend the ships they served on (including helping man the ship's guns when needed). Yet, during this time, the Marines exhibited the remarkable flexibility and adaptability that has come to characterize the Marine Corps, in that they also assisted ably in numerous shore expeditionary actions, helped guard Union supply bases along the coast and rivers, capturing forts, and other tasks.

The Confederate Marines did exist, but were a miniscule part of their military resources (less than 600 officers and men during the entire war). They mainly were stationed on board C.S. Navy ships to assist with defense of the ship, shipboard security, and other shipboard operations, and billeted on shore fortifications to assist with their manpower or security needs.

U.S. Marines in dress uniforms. Library of Congress, Prints & Photographs Division, Civil War Photographs, LC-B817-7697.

The Confederate Cruisers

On April 17, 1861 (two days prior to Lincoln's declaration of a blockade), CSA President Jefferson Davis issued a proclamation authorizing privateering against Union commercial shipping by southern vessel owners. This authorization was subsequently ratified by the Confederate Congress. Commerce raiding was often the strategy used by an inferior navy against a superior one; and this was in fact the strategy used by the U.S. Navy against the British in the Revolutionary War and the War of 1812. The Confederate privateers were the first southern naval offensive of the Civil War against the Union.

As noted earlier in this chapter, the Confederacy eventually decided to conduct commerce raiding using commissioned C.S. Navy warships. Part of the rationale behind this decision was to honor an international treaty barring the practice of privateering (which the United States was not a party to), in hopes of currying favor with European nations who would intervene in the war and assist the Confederacy. Part of the reason also was that the establishment of the Union blockade prevented privateers from sending their captured prizes into southern ports, and the European nations would not allow adjudication of the prizes in their ports. Notable Confederate Navy raiders were the CSS *Sumter*, under the command of Raphael Semmes, the CSS *Florida*, under the command of John Newland Maffit, the CSS *Alabama*, under the command of Semmes after the *Sumter* was sold, and the CSS *Shenandoah*, under the command of James I. Waddell.

One of the rebel privateers that did enjoy great success early in the war was a fast sailing brig converted into the privateer CS *Jefferson Davis*. Under the command of Capt. Louis M. Coxetter, she terrorized Union shipping between June and August 1861. Armed with five ancient English guns, and a crew of 75, well armed with small arms and cutlasses, the *Davis* captured prize after prize, sending them back to Charleston, South Carolina for adjudication before the U.S. Navy blockade closed that port. The "*Jeff Davis*" ended her career wrecked off St. Augustine Florida during a gale. Recent underwater archaeological work in the area appears to have found her remains, and they are currently being explored and recovered. After making their way ashore at St. Augustine, Coxetter and his men were transported to and feted by the people of Jacksonville as true Confederate heroes. Coxetter earned a reputation for treating the officers and crews of his captured vessels in an exceptionally decent manner, and went on to earn greater glory in the war as a captain of blockade runners.

Chapter 2. The Naval War in Florida and the Start of the Civil War

General Overview – Florida and the Navies at the Start of the War

Because of its extensive coastline and remoteness, the leadership of the Confederacy decided early in the war not to expend military resources defending Florida. Many of the Confederate Army regiments formed in the state were withdrawn and deployed to other theatres by the middle of 1862. Few Confederate Navy gunboats or other of their naval resources were invested in the state. The U.S. Army devoted most of its man power and resources to fighting Lee in Virginia and in the western theatre along the Mississippi for the first half of the war. The U.S. Navy, however, was a significant presence in Florida from the beginning, establishing bases early on at Fernandina, Mayport Mills (St. Johns River), St. Augustine, Key West, Egmont Key (Tampa Bay), Seahorse Key (Cedar Keys), and Pensacola. Although I have not seen any specific source or scholar state this, the available evidence indicates (or at least strongly suggests) that the U.S. Navy was the major Union military presence in Florida during the first half of the war.

After the fall of Vicksburg in July 1863, the Union was in complete control of the Mississippi River, the "Father of Waters," from Union territory to the Gulf of Mexico. The trans-Mississippi states of Arkansas, Louisiana, and Texas were cut off from the rest of the Confederacy. The loss of Texas was a particularly critical blow, as it was a major supplier of beef for the Confederate armies. Historians Robert Taylor, Nick Wynne, and Joe Crankshaw indicate that Florida's importance as the breadbasket of the Confederacy, especially as a supplier of beef, increased greatly following Union conquest of the Mississippi. Other vital supplies from Florida included naval stores (turpentine, gum, rosin, etc), salt, lumber, vegetables, cotton, and tobacco.

Because of the decision to essentially abandon Florida, supplemented by the lack of major ports such as Charleston, Savannah, or Mobile, the Confederate Navy never had a presence in Florida. Some rebel gunboats were stationed on the Apalachicola/Chattahoochee River system, mainly to protect the important industrial hub at Columbus, Georgia, and the vital transport route this river system provided (Chapter 3). Many small southern steamboats plied the rivers and coastal waters of Florida, but these were not commissioned

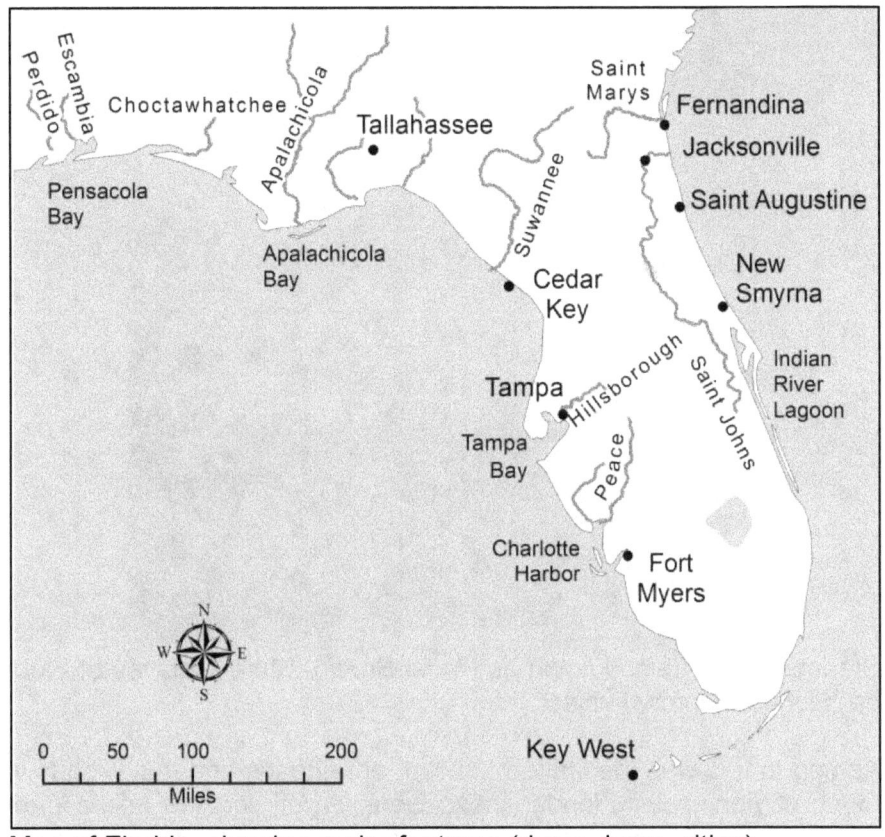

Map of Florida, showing major features (rivers, bays, cities).

warships with the C.S. Navy, although some were impressed into service by and for the Confederate government. After secession, many river steamboats (and their owners/captains) were converted into blockade runners, either running contraband goods between Florida and the Bahamas or "coastal blockade running" between ports in Florida, Georgia, and the Carolinas.

There is some ambiguity over Florida's importance as a destination for blockade runners during the war. Some writers have asserted that Florida was ideal for runners due to its numerous remote inlets, embayment's, and river mouths, offering many points of ingress and egress that could elude the blockade. Others have indicated that the extremely shallow depths of most of these rendered them impassable to all but the smallest of vessels, which severely limited the tonnage of cargo that could be brought in to or out of the state, and that what was brought in contributed little to the overall Confederate war effort.

Steamer *Hattie* (also known as *Hattie Brock*). State Archives of Florida, Florida Memory Project.

Adding to this was the limited network of railroads and main roads in much of peninsular Florida; these were largely located in the panhandle and northern peninsula. This hampered the ability to transport and distribute the materials that were brought in by runners to parts of the Confederacy where they were needed. Even so, blockade running into Florida continued until the very end of the war, and was a boost to southerners' morale.

Takeover of Coastal Fortifications in Florida

The coastal fortifications around Florida were, at the time, believed to be the main defense against naval actions against the state. Confederate forces occupied most of these during the first months of 1861, after Florida's secession, as war loomed. A number of significant naval actions in the subsequent years of the war in Florida occurred in association with these forts, so here I provide an overview of the takeover of the major facilities. Pensacola and Key West will be treated separately.

Ft. Clinch, Fernandina, as it appears today. Author's photo.

Ft. Clinch was located at the mouth of the St. Mary's River, on Cumberland Sound. Construction of this fort began in 1847. The masonry fort was named for Gen. Duncan L. Clinch, a hero of the Seminole Wars in Florida. The fort protected the natural deepwater port of Fernandina, the mouth of the St. Mary's River, and the eastern terminus of the first (and at the time only) cross-state railroad in Florida (Fernandina to Cedar Keys). It was part of the "Third System" of coastal fortifications on the U.S. east coast. At the outbreak of the Civil War, Ft. Clinch was still a work in progress and was not yet completed. Confederate forces occupied the fort sometime between April-June 1861. After great Union victories in the western theatre in February 1862 (the capture of Forts Henry and Donelson by a joint U.S. Army/Navy force), most Confederate military forces in Florida were withdrawn at the orders of Gen. Robert E. Lee, who at the time commanded the coastal defenses in S. Carolina, Georgia, and Florida. The withdrawn Florida troops were sent out west to join the armies of the Confederacy there, or north to eventually serve with Lee in Virginia.

Ft. Marion, at St. Augustine, was a much older facility than Ft. Clinch, dating back to the time of Spanish possession of Florida. It was named for Francis Marion, the "swamp fox" hero of the American

The "sally port" (fort entrance) at Ft. Marion, St. Augustine. State Archives of Florida, Florida Memory Project.

Revolutionary War. The fort was constructed of an unusual limestone material called "coquina"; an amalgam of tiny shells and the remains of other marine organisms mined from a nearby quarry on Anastasia Island. This material was remarkably resistant to solid shot from cannon, in that instead of shattering, as harder rock would do, it simply absorbed the energy of the impact, similar to earthen fortifications. In January 1861, when Florida seceded from the Union, the fort was manned by a tiny garrison of U.S. Army troops (some accounts say only a single sergeant). On January 7, they evacuated and turned it over to Confederate control.

Ft. Brooke, Tampa was first established in 1824. It was initially a campsite of companies of the 4th U.S. Infantry, under the command of Brevet Col. George Mercer Brooke. The fort that was eventually constructed consisted of a wood stockade. It was located at the mouth of the Hillsborough River where it empties into the northern portion of Hillsborough Bay, a branch of larger Tampa Bay. The fort was initially constructed to house U.S. Army troops during the Seminole wars, to protect the citizens of the then small village of Tampa. At the beginning of the Civil War, Confederate militia took possession of Ft. Brooke, and it remained in Confederate hands for much of the

Ft. Brooke, Tampa. State Archives of Florida, Florida Memory Project.

war. A number of other Seminole War era forts were located throughout the state; examples include Ft. Shannon, at Palatka, Ft. Foster, north of Tampa near the Hillsborough River, Ft. Fanning, on the lower Suwannee River, and Ft. Myers in southwest Florida. Some of these were occupied at various times by both Union and Confederate forces during the course of the war.

Florida Lighthouses

Lighthouses on the Florida coast were extremely important aids to navigation for coastal vessels. The term "lighthouse" refers to the tower itself with the light, "light station" is the tower and any accessory structures such as the keepers' residences, workshops, etc. Many of us know Gen. George Gordon Meade as the Union's hero of Gettysburg, as he commanded the Union armies at that iconic engagement. Prior to the war a younger Lt. Meade served in the U.S. Army Engineers where he designed, supervised, and/or was otherwise involved in the construction or modification of seven Florida lighthouses (Carysfort Reef, Sand Key, Seahorse Key, Cape Florida,

Seahorse Key light station, Cedar Keys. State Archives of Florida, Florida Memory Project.

Sombrero Key, Jupiter Inlet, and the first light on Rebecca Shoal). Meade was one of the creators of the screw pile method of anchoring the Florida Keys lights (including Carysfort Reef, Sombrero Key, and Sand Key) in which the foundations for the metal tower were embedded deeply within the limestone of the coral reefs to enable the structure to withstand the force of hurricanes.

Of the thirty three lighthouses/light stations currently in Florida, twenty were in existence at the start of the Civil War (plus one light ship). Before the war, all lighthouses were federal property, administered by a local Superintendent under the Treasury Department. After the southern states' secession and the formation of the CSA, the Confederate Congress created a Confederate Lighthouse Bureau, to be commanded by a senior officer in the Confederate Navy (Captain or Commander). Partly because he happened to be in Montgomery, Alabama at the time (the capital of the CSA at the start of the war), Raphael Semmes was appointed to command the Confederate Lighthouse Bureau; prior to this he served as the naval secretary to the U.S. Light House Board until resigning his naval commission to join the Confederacy. Semmes' tenure in this post was about one week, ending on April 18, after the firing on Ft. Sumter, when he departed to begin fitting out the commerce raider CSS *Sumter*. Seven lighthouses, mainly the ones in the Florida Keys and off Key West, remained in Union hands throughout the war and continued in operation.

Thomas Martin succeeded Semmes as Clerk of the Lighthouse Bureau. By the latter half of 1861, he was overseeing the systematic effort to extinguish all Florida lighthouses under Confederate control and sequester critical components (mainly the lenses and the fuel that fired the light) with the optimistic hope they could be retrieved and reinstalled following the war to guide Confederate commerce. Florida lighthouses witnessed a number of naval actions during the war. The lights at Seahorse Key, Mayport Mills, and Egmont Key (off the mouth of Tampa Bay) were captured by Union Navy forces early in the war. The tower at Pensacola was struck by Union shells a few times during the massive artillery duel in November 1861. The Confederate fort adjacent to the St. Marks lighthouse was engaged by Union gunboats in June 1862 (in retaliation for an attack on a Union shore party a few weeks earlier), and served as a landing site for army forces in 1865 in what eventually was the Battle of Natural Bridge. Seahorse Key and Egmont Key both served as important secondary bases for the East Gulf Blockading Squadron.

Pensacola Navy Yard – 1861

Some considered the Pensacola Navy Yard to be second only to Virginia's Gosport (Norfolk) Navy Yard in importance, and it was the largest navy base on the U.S. Gulf coast. Confederate forces occupied the Navy Yard and adjacent Forts Barrancas and McRee in January 1861, shortly after Florida's secession. Just prior to that occupation, in a maneuver strikingly similar to Maj. Robert Anderson's move out to Ft. Sumter, U.S. Army Lt. Adam J. Slemmer transferred his small garrison of 57 men to Ft. Pickens, on Santa Rosa Island at the mouth of Pensacola Bay. The garrison was supported by 30 sailors, the supply ship USS *Supply* and the gunboat USS *Wyandotte*. *Wyandotte* was the converted merchant steamer *Western Port*. Purchased by the U.S. Navy in 1859, prior to the war, she was chartered to assist with survey operations on the Parana River in South America. She was armed with four 32-pdr smoothbore guns and a 24-pdr Dalhgren boat howitzer. She sailed into the Pensacola Navy Yard in December 1860 for maintenance and was fortuitously present at the outbreak of hostilities. The firepower of the *Wyandotte* was a significant deterrent to the rebels taking military action against the fort early on in the war. Slemmer steadfastly refused several requests by Confederate officers to surrender the fort. In early February 1861, addiadditional reinforcements arrived in the form of the sailing frigate USS *Sabine*, the steam sloop USS *Brooklyn*, and the sailing sloop USS *St. Louis*.

Steam gunboat USS *Wyandotte*. Artwork by Erik Heyl from Naval History and Heritage Command.

Tensions in the area were such that the Civil War could easily have begun in Pensacola, with a firing on Ft. Pickens, rather than Ft. Sumter, South Carolina, but an informal truce with the Union brokered by Confederate Col. William H. Chase and C.S. Navy Secretary Mallory, was agreed to by both sides. The agreement stipulated that food could be brought to Ft. Pickens, but not additional troops or arms. After taking office, Sec. Welles and President Lincoln rejected this and ordered that the garrison at Ft. Pickens be reinforced, and in April, additional Union troops were landed. The steam sloop USS *Powhatan*, under the command of Navy Lt. David Dixon Porter, brought in needed supplies, including arms and ammunition (interestingly, *Powhatan* was supposed to be bound for Ft. Sumter, but was diverted by Sec. Seward counter to the orders of Sec. Welles). Through most of the summer of 1861, things were quiet in Pensacola, but the situation would change by the fall of that year.

The Pensacola Navy Yard as seen from Ft. Pickens. State Archives of Florida, Florida Memory Project.

Landing of reinforcements at Ft. Pickens in April 1861. State Archives of Florida, Florida Memory Project.

Key West, Headquarters of the East Gulf Blockading Squadron

The East Gulf Blockading Squadron headquarters was Key West, Florida, which always remained in Union hands; it never had to be re-taken by Union forces. Back in those days, the only way to get to Key West was by sea. The overseas railroad across the Florida Keys, built by Henry Flagler, and the later overseas highway that was the old "US 1" were decades away. Key West had a U.S. Navy base, and was guarded by Ft. Zachary Taylor on the main island (named for the former President) and Ft. Jefferson, offshore on the Dry Tortugas (also named for the former President and national founder). At the outbreak of the war, the U.S. Navy was thoroughly in control of the base and forts at Key West, and the local southern sympathizers had no way of wresting these from the Union forces.

Ft. Zachary Taylor, Key West. State Archives of Florida, Florida Memory Project.

The East Gulf Squadron had low priority for the U.S. Navy throughout the War, mainly because there were no major ports such as Wilmington, Charleston, Mobile or New Orleans, and thus little potential for major action. It was "the backwater" for USN personnel assigned to ships in the squadron. Yellow fever and malaria were constant plagues on the men who served there. Commander Percival Drayton, on his way from the South Atlantic Squadron over to the West Gulf Squadron to serve as Farragut's Flag Captain, commented on his time in Key West (to a friend in the north):

> *This is rather a dreary residence I should suppose, a sand bank varied with cocoa nut and a few other trees of the tropics, but the soil so light and sandy, as to be almost unfit for gardening purposes, and for all such products as the ordinary table vegetables your city affords their only supply, . . .*

Despite the unspectacular nature of the duty, the efforts of the sailors and marines of the East Gulf Blockading Squadron significantly contributed to the overall success of the Union blockade, as much as those of any of the other squadrons. Shore party raids on salt works crippled salt production, with ripple effects throughout the southern economy and war effort. Cooperation with, and support for, sympathetic Unionists were also important contributions. The squadron organized a group of white Unionists into the Second Florida Cavalry, U.S., which conducted numerous guerilla raids into the interior of the state to interfere with the roundup of Florida beef cattle and other actions. The East Gulf Squadron also formed a regiment of escaped slaves into the Second Infantry Regiment, USCT ("U.S. Colored Troops") to bolster Army forces in the state.

The Navy War in Florida was a River War

An article in the Washington Post stated,". . . the Civil War was a river war." This very much describes the role of the U.S. Navy in Florida during the war, and to a great extent we can say the same thing; the naval war in Florida was very much a river war. For most of the conflict, Confederate Army forces and home guard militia controlled much of the interior of the state (roads and railroads), so the U.S. Army depended on the Navy and leased civilian transport steamers to transport their men, animals, and material along the coasts and via the rivers of the state. Numerous cutting out expeditions to go after blockade runners and/or contraband were conducted up Florida rivers by the U.S. Navy and Army on both coasts in Florida.

Even fictional accounts highlight the river war; in the novel "At the Edge of Honor" by Robert Macomber, a Union Navy armed sloop commanded by Acting Master Peter Wake engages in a nighttime firefight with two Confederate blockade runners on the Peace River, in southwest Florida. Macomber's account captures the intensity, confusion, and terror of close-contact river war:

PHALANX RIVER PICKETS DEFENDING THEMSELVES.
Federal picket boat near Fernandina, Fla., attacked by Confederate sharpshooters stationed in the trees on the banks.

Union gunboat engaging Confederate snipers, possibly on the Amelia River near Fernandina. State Archives of Florida, Florida Memory Project.

> Now they could get a bearing on the enemy sounds, coming down the southern shore of the river, to the right of the **Rosalie,** and almost dead ahead of Thorton's boat. . . Without warning, a blast exploded on the right, followed by a volley of more blasts, as the men in Thorton's boat fired at the enemy. The light of the musket blasts flared out over the water and illuminated the (enemy) schooner for a brief moment. . . . Men on all the vessels were now shouting and screaming. Blasts and flames were coming from everywhere. . . Wake, seeing that the schooner was now just about at the line of anchored vessels and was firing into Thorton's boat, stood up and

yelled as loud as he could, 'Fire, Durlon, fire!' The roar of the twelve-pounder overwhelmed all other noise and action. The flame it spewed out carried for twenty feet and lit up the entire river, clearly showing the damage along the starboard side of the schooner from the dozens of small rounds that had been packed into the canister ammunition. . . . The sound of the screaming and yelling and shooting from the schooner made it sound like a ship from hell as it continued out of control toward Wake's sloop.

The Blockade comes to Florida

Probably because of its importance as a cotton port (Chapter 3), the blockade was established off Apalachicola fairly early in the war, in June 1861, with the arrival of the steam gunboat USS *Montgomery*, under the command of Commander T.D. Shaw. In August 1861, the steam gunboat USS *R.R. Cuyler* joined *Montgomery* and the two gunboats patrolled the waters off Apalachicola Bay and the adjacent Gulf. Both were former merchant steamers purchased by the Navy and converted into gunboats. They were both "screw" steamers, driven by a propeller beneath the stern of the ship. The *Montgomery*

Photo # NH 63883 Steamship Montgomery, which was USS Montgomery during the Civil War

Steam gunboat USS *Montgomery*. Artwork by Erik Heyl from Naval History and Heritage Command.

mounted four 32-pdrs and an 8" rifle, the *Cuyler* was armed with eight 32-pdr guns and two rifled guns. The *Cuyler* was under the command of Capt. Francis B. Ellison.

Steam gunboat USS *R.R. Cuyler*. Artwork by Erik Heyl from Naval History and Heritage Command.

In the early part of December 1861, Flag Officer Samuel F. Du Pont, commanding the South Atlantic Blockading Squadron, ordered Commander Charles Steedman of the side-wheel steam gunboat USS *Bienville* to take up station off St. Simon's Sound, Georgia. *Bienville* was built in New York in 1860 as a merchant steamer and

Steam gunboat USS *Bienville*. Artwork by Erik Heyl from Naval History and Heritage Command.

was purchased by the U.S. Navy in August 1861. Armed with eight 32-pdr smoothbore guns and a 30-pdr rifled gun, she was commissioned with the South Atlantic Squadron in October 1861.

As part of this patrol, Steedman also cruised south to the mouth of the St. Johns River, Florida. On December 11, the *Bienville* sighted two blockade runners, under sail off the mouth of the river. Her crew captured the pilot schooner *Sarah and Caroline*, and the other runner was driven ashore. The captured runner carried 60 barrels of turpentine and was evidently bound for Nassau, Bahamas. The blockade was now officially imposed off the east coast of Florida.

Union Navy Officers in Florida

Commander Daniel Ammen. Appointed a Midshipman in the U.S. Navy in July 1836, Ammen served as an officer on the USS *Roanoke*, in the North Atlantic Blockading Squadron, at the beginning of the war. He was then given command of the USS *Seneca*, in the South Atlantic Squadron. It was during this command that he served in the Florida theatre, participating in the occupation of Fernandina and operations on the St. Johns River. He retired in 1877 as an Admiral and authored the book "The Atlantic Coast", part of the 1883 series "The Navy in the Civil War."

Admiral Daniel Ammen, after the war. Naval History and Heritage Command.

Acting Volunteer Lieutenant I. B. Baxter. Joined the Navy as a volunteer officer in August 1861. He eventually commanded the bark *Gem of the Sea*, serving in the East Gulf Blockading Squadron, and saw service off both the southeast and southwest coasts of Florida. He was honorably discharged in December 1865.

Acting Master (later Lt.) William R. Browne. Was appointed Acting Master as a volunteer officer in May 1861. He resigned this commission later that year, but at some point must have re-enlisted as an Acting Master, as he was a participant in a number of salt works raids in St. Andrews Bay the latter part of 1863. He was promoted to Acting Volunteer Lieutenant in February 1864. He was honorably discharged from naval service at the end of the war in 1865.

Acting Ensign Edwin Crissey. Enlisted in the U.S. Navy in January 1863 as a volunteer officer (Acting Ensign). He was promoted to Acting Master in June 1864. He may have been one of the rare few offered a permanent commission in the USN due to his outstanding efforts during the war, because records indicate he resigned his commission in 1865 at the war's end, as opposed to being discharged. He re-enlisted in the Navy as a Petty Officer in January 1873 and retired from the service in 1894.

Commander Percival Drayton. A native of South Carolina, Percival Drayton joined the U.S. Navy in December 1827 as a Midshipman. He did not resign his commission at the start of the war

Commander Percival Drayton. Naval History and Heritage Command.

to join the southern effort and remained a loyal Union man with the U.S. Navy. At Port Royal, South Carolina, he was in command of the USS *Pocahontas* when he engaged the guns of Fort Walker, which was commanded by his brother, Confederate Gen. Thomas F. Drayton. He participated in the Union retaking of Ft. Clinch and occupation of Fernandina, Florida, commanding the steam sloop USS *Pawnee*. After that, he commanded the ironclad monitor USS *Passaic* in the engagement with Ft. McAllister, Georgia. He was subsequently assigned as Flag Captain to Adm. David Farragut of the West Gulf Blockading Squadron. He died in August 1865.

Lt. Commander Earl English. Received appointment as a Midshipman in February 1840. He was promoted to Lt. Commander in July 1862 and saw service on both coasts of Florida during the war, in the East Gulf Blockading Squadron, commanding the converted New York ferryboat USS *Somerset* and then the *Unadilla*-Class gunboat USS *Sagamore*. He continued to serve in the Navy after the war and retired at the rank of Rear Admiral in 1884.

Lt. Commander David B. Harmony. Enlisted in the U.S. Navy in 1847 as a Midshipman. He was promoted to Lt. Commander in July 1862. He was an officer on the ironclad monitor USS *Nahant* when she accompanied her sister gunboat USS *Weehawken* in the battle with the Confederate ironclad CSS *Atlanta* on the Georgia coast, and was in command of the boarding party that took possession of the rebel warship after her defeat. He commanded the gunboat USS *Tahoma* in 1864, patrolling the waters off the eastern panhandle and upper Big Bend of Florida. He retired as a Rear Admiral in 1893.

Commander John C. Howell. He entered the Navy in June 1836 and was promoted to Commander in July 1862. He was involved in operations off the Florida Gulf coast during much of the war in the East Gulf Blockading Squadron. He remained in the Navy after the war and was promoted to flag rank in April 1877. He retired in 1881.

Acting Lieutenant Edward Yorke McCauley. McCauley was commissioned in the Navy as a Midshipman in September 1841. He was an officer serving under Commodore Matthew Perry on the U.S. Navy's historic mission to Japan to try to open relations with the U.S. in 1852-54. He served in the U.S. Navy until 1859, when he resigned his commission due to ill health and a general disillusionment with service in the Navy. When the Civil War broke out, McCauley re-enlisted and was appointed Acting Lieutenant. He was placed in command of the newly purchased and refitted New York ferryboat USS *Fort Henry*, serving in the East Gulf Blockading Squadron. Afterward, he also served in vessels on the Mississippi River. He continued to serve in the Navy after the war and retired in 1887 with the rank of Rear Admiral.

Commander Christopher Raymond Perry Rogers. C.R.P. Rogers was appointed a Midshipman in October 1833. At the beginning of the war, he was Commandant of the U.S. Naval Academy and over-

Commander C.R.P. Rogers. Library of Congress, Prints & Photographs Division, Civil War Photographs, LC-B813-3803-A.

saw its temporary relocation. He was then commissioned a Commander, and served as captain of the USS *Wabash* for a period of time during its service as flagship of the South Atlantic Blockading Squadron. He was eventually appointed a staff officer to Rear Adm. Du Pont. He retired as a Rear Admiral in 1881, after serving a second stint as Superintendant of the Naval Academy.

Commander Charles Steedman. Charles Steedman joined the Navy as a Midshipman in April 1828. A southerner by birth, he remained loyal to the Union. At the war's outbreak, he held the rank of Commander, and as captain of the USS *Bienville* was involved in initial blockade efforts off northeast Florida. He was the senior naval officer in charge of the Navy flotilla that engaged the Confederate battery at St. Johns Bluff in fall 1862, commanding the side-wheel steam gunboat USS *Paul Jones*. He retired from the Navy as a Rear Admiral in May 1871.

Lieutenant Thomas Holdup Stevens. Yet another Union officer with roots in the south, his father was a renowned naval officer in the War of 1812 and in a long career with the U.S. Navy. Stevens received an appointment as a Midshipman in the Navy in December

1836. He was given command of the USS *Ottawa* at the beginning of the war in 1861. He participated in actions taking Ft. Clinch and the Port of Fernandina and was involved in St. Johns River operations throughout much of 1862 in service with the South Atlantic Blockading Squadron. The latter part of that year, he was transferred to the East Gulf Blockading Squadron where he was involved in the blockade off the Florida Keys. He retired as a Rear Admiral in October 1879.

Acting Master Edmund C. Weeks. Joined the Navy in September 1861 as a volunteer officer. Weeks served under Lt. Cdr. David Harmony on the USS *Tahoma*, where he was instrumental in helping forge ties with local Unionists and organizing them into a raiding party that became the Second Florida Cavalry, US. He eventually resigned his USN commission to join the U.S. Army, who commissioned him a Major to command the Second Fla. Cavalry, U.S. In September 1864 Weeks was relieved of his command and sent to Key West to be court marshaled under a number of charges. He was cleared of all charges and resumed command of the cavalry regiment in early 1865. He was in command of a party of Union troops at the Battle of Natural Bridge.

Commander Maxwell Woodhull. Entered the Navy as a Midshipman in June 1832. He was appointed a Commander in July 1861

Edmund C. Weeks, USN and USA. State Archives of Florida, Florida Memory Project.

and served in operations on the St. Johns River through much of the latter part of 1862, commanding the gunboat USS *Cimarron*. He was accidentally killed by the explosion of a ceremonial gun in February 1863.

Confederate Navy Officers in Florida

    Lt. George W. Gift. Gift entered the U.S. Navy as a Midshipman in 1847. He resigned his commission only a few years later, in 1851, to go into business for himself on the west coast of the U.S. Gift had served with Catesby ap Roger Jones in the Pacific. After the southern states' secession, he traveled from California to join the C.S. Navy. He served for a period of time on the ironclad CSS *Arkansas* on the Mississippi River and even caught the attention of Adm. Franklin Buchanan, who regarded him highly. He served as an officer on the gunboat CSS *Chattahoochee* in Georgia and Florida in 1863, and was a participant in the CSN raid on the Union gunboat USS *Underwriter* in New Bern, North Carolina in early 1864. He then returned to Florida and was placed in command of the CSS *Chattahoochee* later in 1864 after it was raised and repaired and was involved in actions on the Apalachicola River and Bay.
    Lt. John J. Guthrie. Joined the USN as a Midshipman in 1834. He rose to the rank of Lieutenant by 1847. Records indicate he was dismissed from the Navy in July 1861, probably after he had submitted his resignation to head south. Sec. Welles was so furious at the resignations, he ended up dismissing from the service any officers who submitted or indicated they were submitting their resignation. He took command of the CSS *Chattahoochee* after C. ap R. Jones moved on to other duties. He was in command of the gunboat when her boilers blew up on the Apalachicola River in May 1863.
    Lt. Catesby ap Roger Jones. Entered the Navy in 1836 as a Midshipman. By 1849 he had been promoted to Lieutenant. He resigned his commission in April 1861 to join the southern war effort as an officer in the C.S. Navy. As the CSS *Virginia's* Executive Officer, he took command of the warship on 9 March after Adm. Franklin Buchanan was injured by a musket ball, and was in command of the rebel ironclad in the historic engagement with the USS *Monitor* that day. Eventually he was assigned to help oversee the fitting out of the CSS *Chattahoochee* in Saffold, Georgia and was the first commander of that gunboat. At the war's end, he was in command of CSN gunboat construction efforts in the Mobile/Selma area.

Lt. Catesby ap Roger Jones, CSN. Naval History and Heritage Command.

Lt. Charles P. McGary. Entered the Navy as a Midshipman in 1841. He rose to the rank of Lieutenant by 1855. He resigned his commission in April 1861 to join the C.S. Navy and the southern war effort. He commanded the gunboat CSS *Spray* on the St. Marks River and was involved in negotiations with the commander of the USS *Kingfisher* to parole Union sailors captured by the rebels in a watering expedition up the Aucilla River.

Lt. Augustus McLaughlin. Was appointed a Midshipman in 1840. He was dismissed from the Navy for a period of time due to drunkenness, but was eventually reinstated and saw service in the Mexican War and afterward serving on various supply ships, which gave him a superb grasp of logistics. At the beginning of the Civil War, he resigned his USN commission and joined the C.S. Navy. He was initially involved in the construction of land batteries at Apalachicola. He transferred from this service to supervise and oversee construction of gunboats for the C.S. Navy at Saffold and Columbus, Georgia. He also helped coordinate and supply CSN gunboat construction efforts at other ports, including Savannah, Charleston, Selma and Wilmington.

Chapter 3. Actions in the Panhandle 1861-1864

Pensacola Bay and the Pensacola Navy Yard

The summer of 1861 passed quietly at Pensacola, with the Confederates reinforcing their positions on the mainland and Union forces fortifying their garrison at Ft. Pickens, on Santa Rosa Island. Because the Union position effectively sealed off use of the Navy Yard and Pensacola Bay from the adjacent Gulf of Mexico, the seizure of the Navy Yard never really benefitted the Confederacy. In late August, a rebel vessel attempted to put to sea from the Navy Yard, but gunfire from Union batteries erected on Santa Rosa turned it back.

U.S. Navy flotilla supporting Ft. Pickens, Pensacola, in early 1861. Naval History and Heritage Command.

The Union garrison at Ft. Pickens was first supported by the Union gunboat USS *Wyandotte* (already present at Pensacola at the outbreak of hostilities). In February 1861, a flotilla of USN warships arrived to support the garrison, consisting of the sailing frigate USS *Sabine*, the steam sloop USS *Brooklyn*, and the sailing sloop USS *St. Louis*. Of these, the *Brooklyn* was the newest and most formidable warship. A member of the *Hartford*-Class of steam sloop warships, she was a sister ship to Farragut's famous flagship. She was completed in 1858 and commissioned in 1859 and was powered by a square-rigged sail plan and a steam engine that drove a screw (propeller) beneath the stern of the ship. Her gun deck armament consisted of 20 9" smoothbore guns mounted in broadside and a 10" smoothbore gun in pivot.

Burning of the dry dock in Pensacola Bay. State Archives of Florida, Florida Memory Project.

In early September, a Union Navy raiding party burned a dry dock that had floated loose in Pensacola Bay to prevent its recovery and use by the Confederates. About this same time, Flag Officer Mervine of the Gulf Blockading Squadron received a report that the Confederates were fitting out the privateer CS *Judah* at the Pensacola Yard. During the night of September 13-14, 1861, a raiding force of 100 bluejackets and marines under Lt. John H. Russell set out from Mervine's flagship, the USS *Colorado*.

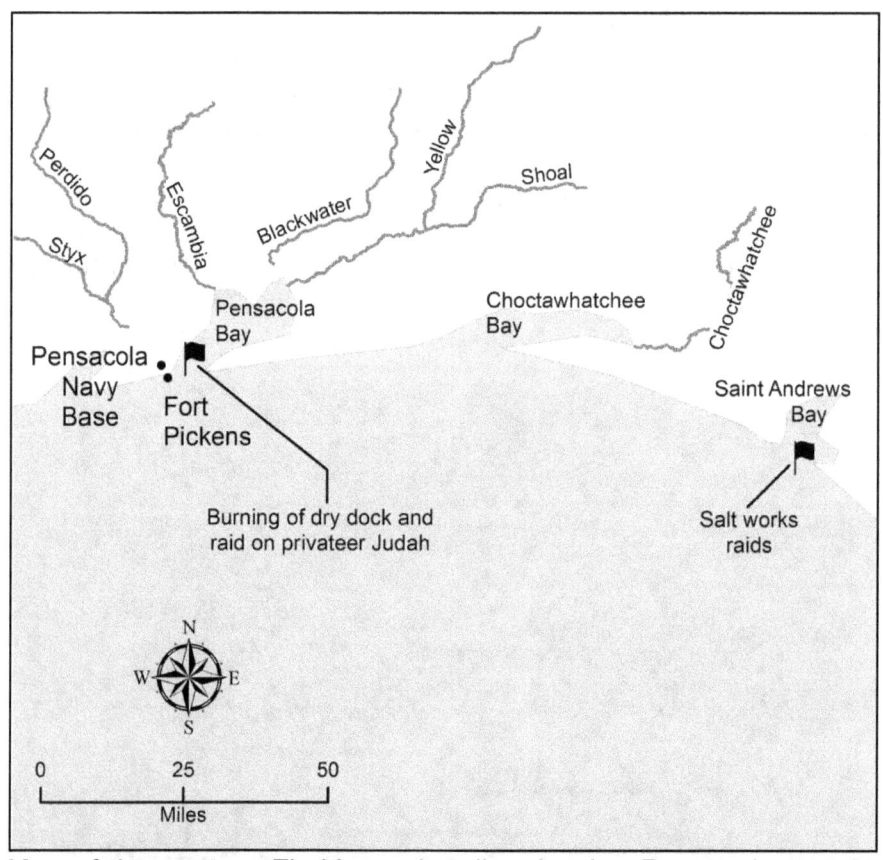

Map of the western Florida panhandle, showing Pensacola and St. Andrews Bays and naval events.

Somehow, the Confederate watch on the *Judah* had been forewarned, and they opened fire on the Union sailors. Undaunted, the sailors and marines swarmed over the gunwales and captured the privateer. Confederate reinforcements arrived on the adjacent dock and an intense firefight ensued between ship and shore. Russell ordered the spiking of the guns mounted on the privateer, and subsequently set fire to the schooner. The entire affair was over in fifteen minutes, and the Union raiders returned to the *Colorado* with the *Judah* burning away brightly. The Union force suffered three killed and thirteen wounded, the Confederates the same number killed and unknown number of wounded. Historian Dr. Ed Bearss has noted that this was the first Civil War combat engagement in Florida involving loss of life.

Burning of the Confederate privateer CS *Judah* in Pensacola Harbor. State Archives of Florida, Florida Memory Project.

Angered by the Union Navy's raid, Confederate Gen. Braxton Bragg, commanding the C.S. Army forces garrisoning Forts Barrancas and McRee and the Pensacola Navy Yard, sent a force of 1,200 soldiers to Santa Rosa Island. The force landed at night on October 8, 1861 and assaulted the camp of the 6th New York, a Zouave regiment. The Union troops were initially routed, but reinforcements from Ft. Pickens helped them reform and they pushed the Confederate forces back, who departed the island by the next morning.

In response to that attack, and the increasing size of the Confederate force garrisoning Pensacola, Col. Harvey Brown, now commanding the Union forces on Santa Rosa Island, ordered his artillery to open fire on the mainland on November 22, 1861. The Confederates returned the Union gunfire. The army artillery was supplemented by gunfire from the steam frigate USS *Niagara* and steam sloop USS *Richmond*. The *Niagara* was one of the Navy's largest ships, one of the steam-screw frigates, armed with a battery of XI (11)-inch Dahlgren guns. *Richmond* was a sister ship to the *Brooklyn* and *Hartford* and was armed similar to her siblings.

Steam frigate USS *Niagara*. Naval History and Heritage Command.

For two days, the bombardment continued, with thousands of rounds expended by both sides. Ft. McRee was completely destroyed by the gunfire from the U.S. Navy ships, and portions of the Navy Yard and adjacent villages were set on fire from the barrage. USS *Richmond* suffered one sailor killed and seven injured by fire from the Confederate batteries. Hostilities ceased on the night of November 23.

At the beginning of 1862, the Confederates had amassed a force of 16,000 troops in the region, under the command of Major Gen. Bragg. Reinforcements could be brought in by rail from Mobile, Alabama, as needed. In January 1862 another, smaller artillery duel was fought between Union forces on Santa Rosa Island and Confederate gunnery on the mainland. Events out west eventually dictated what the Confederacy would do at Pensacola. In February 1862, Confederate Forts Henry and Donelson fell to the Union, through joint Army/Navy operations. In March 1862, U.S. Navy and Army forces began to move on the Mississippi River, taking ports and important fortifications. Those Union victories forced the Confederacy to have to deploy forces to the western theatre to meet the Union threat.

Bragg was ordered to move his forces westward to bolster the Confederate military effort there. Preparatory to abandoning Pensacola, he ordered his executive officer:

> *I desire you particularly to leave nothing the enemy can use; burn all from Fort McRee to the junction with the Mobile road. Save the guns, and if necessary destroy your gunboats and all other boats. They might be used against us. Destroy all machinery, etc., public and private, which could be useful to the enemy; especially disable the sawmills in and around the bay and burn the lumber. Break up the railroad from Pensacola to the Junction, carrying the iron up to a safe point.*

Another skirmish between Union and Confederate troops was fought between late March and early April 1862 at Pensacola Bay. By then, withdrawal of Confederate forces was in full swing, although surprisingly the Union did not have detailed knowledge of those actions. In early April 1862, Bragg suffered a repulsing and bloody defeat by Gen. U.S. Grant at Shiloh, Tennessee, while later that month, Farragut bypassed Forts St. Philip and Jackson on the Mississippi and took New Orleans. Those Union victories spelled the ultimate doom for any hope of holding on to Pensacola by the Confederacy, as by then the strategic decision had been made to withdraw all Confederate troops from Florida for use elsewhere.

By early May 1862, the evacuation of Pensacola and the Navy Yard was complete. The retreating Confederates set fire to any public property that ". . . *could be of use to the foe.*" Seeing the blaze, the U.S. Army commander at Ft. Pickens dispatched his aide-de-camp and a small force to take possession of the Navy Yard and the town. Navy Commander David D. Porter arrived at this time as well; he saw the blaze from his station off Mobile Bay and knew that the destruction indicated the possible abandonment of the Navy Yard. For the rest of the war, Pensacola remained in Union hands and became the main base of operations for the West Gulf Blockading Squadron. In retrospect, major kudos must go to young Army Lt. Adam J. Slemmer, who steadfastly obeyed his orders and retained possession of Ft. Pickens back in early 1861. Union control of that fort and Santa Rosa Island essentially bottled up the harbor at Pensacola and denied use of its important navy yard by the Confederacy.

St. Andrews Bay and Confederate Salt Works

On March 20, 1863, a landing party from the USS *Roebuck* landed on St. Andrews Bay, near present-day Panama City. Their objective was to attempt to cut out a suspected blockade runner. Acting Master John Sherrill, commanding the *Roebuck*, received intelligence that a ship was loading cotton to run the blockade. He sent a ship's boat with eleven men, under the command of Acting Master James Folger, to proceed up the bay to find and destroy or capture the runner. Unfortunately, the landing party ran into a strong defense by Confederate home guard militia, under the command of Capt. W. J. Robinson of the C.S. Army. Seamen Thomas King and

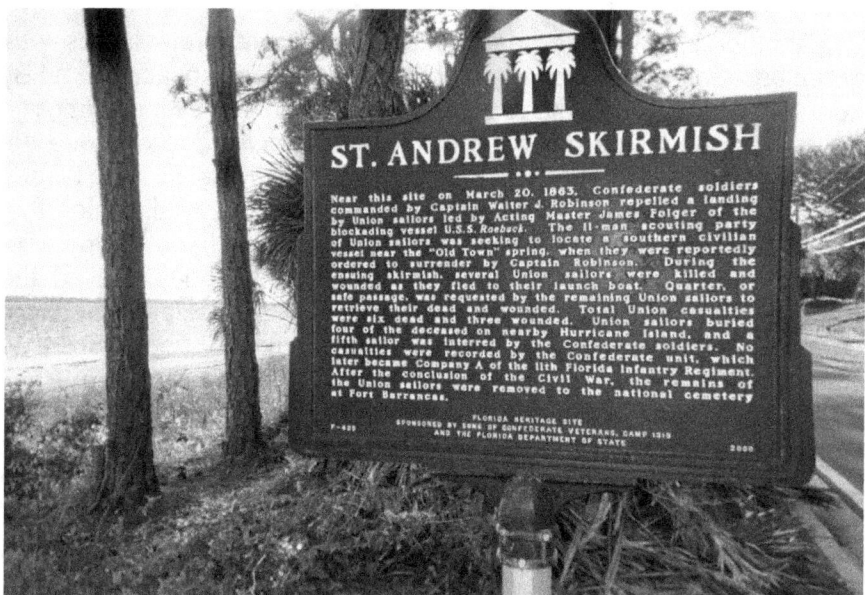

Historic marker in Panama City describing the March 20, 1863 Union Raid. Author's photo.

Ralph B. Snow were killed in that action and seven other sailors were injured, including the landing party commander, Act. Master Folger. The official reports indicate that some of the injured were "severely injured", so perhaps they died later, accounting for the listing of "six dead" on the historic marker. Capt. Sherrill's squadron commander, Adm. Theodorus Bailey, did not approve of the action, and believed it to be "ill-advised".

As the Civil War progressed, salt became one of the most vital commodities for the Confederacy. Salt was the primary means of preserving meat at that time, along with many other critical uses. By the end of 1861, the CSA realized that it required a reliable supply of salt, as the tightening U.S. Navy blockade was beginning to severely cut off imports from Europe. Every year, the states making up the Confederacy required six million bushels of salt, over half of which was imported before the war. Prior to the war, salt sold for 50 cents a sack off the ships at New Orleans; it sold for $25 per sack in Savannah in January 1862. By October of that year, it was selling for $140 per sack in Atlanta. A "sack" typically constituted two or three bushels of salt, the latter being the standard measure. Production of salt became so important that if one worked in a salt works, it gave him an exemption from conscription into the Confederate Army.

While some salt was produced along the coasts of many of the southern states, its remote coastline made Florida the ideal place for that enterprise. Salt production was particularly prolific along Florida's Gulf coast, and a large number of Confederate salt works were established, where sources of saltwater and wood (for stoking fires) were abundant. It eventually became a major task of the Union Navy blockaders to locate and destroy the works, much of that burden falling to the East Gulf Blockading Squadron, responsible for most of the Florida Gulf coast. As runner after runner was captured and its cargo examined, the USN blockaders almost always found salt in the cargoes.

St. Andrews Bay, in the middle of the Florida panhandle, became the epicenter of Florida salt production and a main focus of Union Navy raids. A boat party attempted to destroy salt works and persuade the slaves operating the works to defect to the Union in St. Joseph's and St. Andrews bays in September 1862. They refused to do so at that time, due to suspicions of the motives of the Navy men, but the slaves in the region soon came to realize that the U.S. Navy really was their ticket to freedom and increasingly provided intelligence and cooperated with the USN.

Four slaves reported the occurrence of a salt works near the Cape San Blas lighthouse in February 1862 to officers of the US Bark *Kingfisher*. In September, the bark sailed into St. Joseph Bay and sent a boat ashore under a flag of truce to inform the Confederates that they would begin to destroy the works in two hours. The boat returned to the gunboat and during that time, the bluejackets watched the inhabitants of the works withdraw, carrying as much salt and other goods as they could. After the allotted time, the *Kingfisher* fired three shells into the works to signal the end of the grace period and dispatched a landing party, which destroyed a salt works estimated to produce 200 bushels of salt per day. The landing party returned with chests of carpenters tools and eleven slaves who had requested evacuation. Adm. Lardner wrote in his report, "*The salt works at St. Joseph's* (sic) *Bay, estimated of capacity to make 200 bushels of salt a day, were destroyed by Lieutenant Commanding Couthouy, of the* Kingfisher, *on the 8th of September.*"

After this effort, two Unionists from Georgia requested asylum aboard the *Kingfisher* and told Couthouy that the destruction of the St. Joseph Bay salt works caused great economic distress to the citizens of the region. On September 11, 1862, the USS *Sagamore*

Raid on a Confederate salt works by a landing party from the USS *Kingfisher*. State Archives of Florida, Florida Memory Project.

hove to in St. Andrews Bay and sent boats ashore to destroy a works with an estimated production capacity of 216 bushels per day. On many of those raids, the slaves who worked at the works now willingly assisted in their destruction and departed with the sailors.

The steam gunboat USS *Albatross* served in the West Gulf Blockading Squadron, and mostly operated off the coasts of Mississippi and Louisiana. However, in late 1862, her patrol sector was the area of Florida coast between Pensacola and St. Andrews Bay. In November 1862, her crew conducted a Union Navy raid on the St. Andrews Bay salt works. In his after-action report, Lt. Commander John E. Hart, commanding the *Albatross*, wrote:

On the morning of the 24th November, at 4 a.m., I started off with an expedition under my command in the direction of North Bay. The Bohio *furnished two boats and 30 men, one of the boats having a howitzer; and the* Albatross *armed and equipped three boats with 30, besides a working gang of coal heavers and firemen, with sledge hammers, top mauls, cold chisels and axes.*

We proceeded up an arm of St. Andrew's (sic) Bay, called North Bay, about 12 or 14 miles, and reached a point of land, where we concluded to rest until broad daylight. The bay was very wide at this point, and a fog hung over the water, preventing us from seeing which way to go. As soon as we lay on our oars, we thought we heard voices on shore. Pulling in the direction, we soon ascertained that we were near quite a number of people, and as we came nearer, we not only heard voices, but we heard dogs barking and horses neighing, and we felt

Steam gunboat USS *Albatross*. Sketch by W.M.C. Philbrick. Naval History and Heritage Command.

quite sure that we had stumbled upon a company of cavalry and soldiers, for day was breaking, and what we afterwards found out were canvas-covered wagons, we

> then mistook for tents. I thought I would startle them, and ordered a shell to be sent over their heads, and in a minute there never was heard such shouting and confusion. They seemed not to know which way to run.

Hart noted that eventually the rebels managed to get some of the wagons hooked up and evacuated the area. He directed the boat with the howitzer to occasionally fire a shot in the direction of the fleeing Confederates. The water being too shallow to get the boats up to the beach, the landing party waded ashore about 200 yards through thick mud to get to the works. Hart continued:

> We threw out pickets, and Acting Master Browne, with the men belonging to the *Bohio*, took one direction, and I, with my men and officers, took the other, and, with top mauls, axes, sledge hammers, and shovels, we commenced the destruction of salt kettles and salt pans, and mason work, for we had got into a settlement of salt workers.

The landing party destroyed the salt boilers, ruined the salt already made which had been left at the site, and set fire to structures, sheds, barrels, boxes and wagons. Over the next two weeks, additional salt works between St. Andrews and Pensacola Bays were discovered by the *Albatross* and *Bohio* and were destroyed.

A uniquely different account of the salt works raids comes from Third Assistant Engineer Louis James M. Boyd of the *Albatross*, who wrote his wife:

> The manner in which those Expeditions are arranged are that we would leave the ships about four o'clock in the morning, and proceed up the Bay until we would discover Smoke, for that is the only way that those pans (the salt works boilers) can be found by a stranger. As soon as we would get near enough we would then fire at them with a Small Cannon we have and such Skidaddeling you never seen in your life. They would leave everything behind them. We went in Several of there camps and found there Breakfast cooked and on the Table ready for eating, which our boys would soon demolish, after rowing So early in the Morning. We would then set about breaking up their pans and works. . . .

Boyd may have been in charge of the "coal heavers and firemen" Capt. Hart mentioned, who by virtue of their brawny statures (sort of a requirement of the rating), were tasked with destroying the salt boilers and accoutrements, while armed sailors and marines set up a defensive perimeter.

Interestingly, historian George Buker noted that those initial salt works raids were harassing efforts, conducted incidentally to other blockade activities. The strategic importance of salt to the Confederacy was not apparent to the East Gulf Squadron command until they noted that nearly every blockade runner they captured contained salt as at least a portion of its cargo. It was then that the squadron command realized that a concentrated effort to find and destroy these works would be a major strategic blow to the Confederate war effort. In December 1863 the focused raids began.

On December 2, 1863, the bark USS *Restless*, under the command of Acting Master William R. Browne, sent a landing party in to Lake Ocala in St. Andrews Bay. They found three separate works with a total capacity of 130 bushels per day. The landing party destroyed carts and flat boats, disposed of the salt, and took seventeen prisoners. Due to the fact that they had no room to bring them back to the gunboat, they made the southerners swear an oath of allegiance to not take up arms against the Union, and released them.

Hearing of Browne's exploits, Acting Ensign Edwin Crissey, commanding the steam gunboat USS *Bloomer*, and with the sloop *Caroline*, sought out the *Restless* and offered to assist Browne and his ship. Like the USS *Albatross*, Crissey and his ships were with the West Gulf Blockading Squadron, but his proximity to the East Gulf Squadron's operations area enabled him to help there. On December 10, 1863, the USN flotilla steamed into St. Andrews Bay and split up into two enterprises. Browne fired two shells into the town of St. Andrew to warn the Confederate soldiers and salt workers garrisoned there. He then commenced shelling the town, which shortly was burning. The entire town was destroyed by the fire.

Crissey and his men landed in West Bay and proceeded to the salt works. From his report dated December 20, 1863, he described a major raid on these:

> *At 5 p.m. I proceeded to the salt works on West Bay, destroying the salt works lined on each side of the bay for 7 miles, belonging to private individuals, numbering at least 198 different works, each averaging two boilers and ten kettles each, which, with a large quantity of salt, were destroyed. . . . . On the afternoon of the 14th we came to*

> *a large Confederate Government works, under the command of Mr. Clendening, which turned out daily 400 bushels of salt. This was one of the best located in West Bay, being situated in a marsh, the water of which yielded 75 gallons of salt to 100 gallons of water; it was, in fact, a complete salt village, covering a space of three-fourths of a square mile, employing many hands and 16 ox and mule teams constantly to haul salt to Eufola Sound [Eufaula, Ala?], and from thence conveyed to Montgomery, at which place it is selling at a fabulous price of $40 and $45 per bushel. At this place were 27 buildings, 22 large steam boilers, and 200 kettles, averaging 200 gallons each, which cost the Government $5 per gallon, all of which were totally destroyed, together with storehouses containing salt, etc. This work, together with the other works, could not have cost less than three million dollars.*

On December 18, Browne and some of his men joined Crissey and they proceeded to the salt works on the East Bay. As the boats approached, they saw smoke billowing from the works, due to the rebels setting them on fire before they evacuated. A landing party was sent ashore and the bluejackets destroyed any remaining salt boilers and set fire to the remaining structures on the site. The USN forces also forced the destruction of salt works in the North Bay.

Because of the critical importance of salt, the Confederates immediately rebuilt the salt works in St. Andrews Bay after the Union forces departed. The rebels would not give up! Escaped slaves told Browne about this, and that additional material was being transported down the Wetappo River to build larger works. Browne sent word to Crissey to see if he could come to reestablish their effective partnership. Unfortunately this time, Crissey had orders to stay on his blockading station, so Browne sent in two parties of his own men to again destroy these works. The redoubtable Browne reported on February 17, 1864:

> *Learning that the rebels had erected new Government salt works on West Bay, on the site of the old salt works destroyed by us in December, and that they had a force of 50 men armed and stationed there for protection, I fitted out the first cutter, manned with 13 men, under charge of Acting Ensign James J. Russell, with orders to proceed up the Gulf coast 20 miles, and march inland 7*

miles to the salt works and attack them in the rear, while Acting Ensign Henry Eason with 10 men, in command of the second cutter, would proceed by the inside passage and attack them in the front at the same time.

The expedition was entirely successful, the works being abandoned upon the appearance of our men, Messrs. Russell's and Eason's party joining at the appropriate time, and immediately proceeded in the destruction of everything in the manufactories, consisting of 26 sheet-iron boilers, averaging 881 gallons, and 19 kettles, averaging 200 gallons, making an aggregate of 26,706 gallons, which cost in Montgomery $5.50 per gallon.

In yet another expedition, beginning on March 31, 1864, Browne sent a party of Unionist Floridians up the Wetappo River with three of his men to destroy a Confederate storehouse of salt. Obstructions in the river impeded their progress, but they arrived on April 2 and destroyed the contents, dumping the salt into the river. They also captured the barge used to transport salt and supplies, which Browne renamed the "*Wartappo*" (from its previous name of *Wetappo*). A number of Unionist refugees accompanied the landing party back down river to the gunboat. Browne had the barge modified with a new mast and bowsprit and had a platform mounted on the deck with a 12-pdr howitzer. This very shallow-draft craft became an effective and useful addition to his efforts. Because of his initiative, Browne was promoted to Acting Lieutenant. The Crystal River Boat Builders club is presently building a full-size replica of the *Wartappo* for use in living history and re-enactment events.

In still yet another demonstration of his "never give up" attitude, Browne sent a boat expedition of 22 men into the East Bay to destroy yet another rebuilt salt works. The expedition departed the evening of April 12, 1864. Their objective was to destroy two boats rumored to be in the Bay, and two "large Government salt works." The party did not find the boats (later learning they had been moved to West Bay), but succeeded in finding and destroying the salt works. They also destroyed a storehouse and its contents of 300 bushels of salt, 200 bushels of corn and 50 bushels of meal. The expedition returned to the USS *Restless* with an escaped slave who requested asylum with the Union. Summarizing Browne's report to him, Adm. Bailey wrote:

Acting Volunteer Lieutenant Browne reports that there are five companies of rebel troops in that vicinity to

Naval re-enactors at the 2011 St. Andrews Bay Salt Works Raid event. Photo courtesy Karen Lou Rogers, used by permission.

guard the salt works, and that these works are rebuilt as fast as he destroys them.

A living history event ("St. Andrews Bay Salt Works Raid") is held on a weekend in April in Panama City to educate folks about the importance of salt making to the Confederacy and the many Union attempts to destroy these as described here.

Apalachicola River and Bay

Prior to the war, Apalachicola was a very important cotton port on the Florida Gulf coast, mainly due to the Apalachicola, Flint and Chattahoochee Rivers providing an easy water transport route to the port for steamboats carrying cotton grown in plantations in the Florida panhandle and adjacent south Georgia and southeast Alabama. By 1840, it was third in importance of the cotton ports on the Gulf coast (after New Orleans and Mobile). Apalachicola can be visited today, and you can see a few of the old cotton warehouse buildings remaining along the waterfront.

As noted in Chapter 2, the blockade was established off Apalachicola in mid-1861 with the arrival of the gunboats USS *Montgomery* in June, and *R.R. Cuyler* in August. The *Montgomery* was commanded by Commander T. D. Shaw, and the *Cuyler* by Captain Francis B. Ellison. On his arrival on August 19, Ellison was informed by Commander Shaw that they had been watching the fitting out of a schooner in the bay, presumably to try a run through the blockade. They decided to embark a cutting out expedition to secure the rebel ship. On the night of August 26, two boats from *Montgomery* and three from *Cuyler* set out, under the command of Ellison's second lieutenant James Parker. They boarded and captured the schooner and its crew without incident. The schooner was the *Finland*, whose ownership was dubious because the crew and captain could not produce proper documentation and the schooner's master gave conflicting statements to Lt. Parker and the *Cuyler's* paymaster. The morning of August 28, the USN raiders attempted to get the *Finland* out of the bay and under the protection of the Union gunboats, as Parker believed she was a legitimate prize of war. Weather, tide and shallow depths all conspired to thwart the Union sailors' efforts. The appearance of a small rebel steamer towing a "large schooner" forced Lt. Parker to conclude that they would soon have a fight on their hands. He ordered the *Finland* to be burned and the crew taken prisoner. Ellison reported to Flag Officer Mervine of the Gulf Blockading Squadron:

> *The* Finland *is burned to the water's edge and her destruction is complete. From what I glean from the mates and crew, I have no doubt but that she was being prepared to receive a cargo of cotton, a supply of which is now at Apalachicola, and proposed running the blockade.*
>
> *Steamers had been visiting her with company and provisions before our arrival.*

The *Finland's* first and second mates, carpenter, steward, ship's boy and ten free African Americans all requested permission to join the U.S. Navy. Most appeared to have been competent seamen and Ellison asked Flag Off. Mervine permission to muster them into the service. Ellison then paroled the remaining crew and the schooner's late master at his request. Actions such as these demonstrated to the citizens of the region that the U.S. Navy was there to help them and was not there to implement a reign of terror or destruction.

Florida Gov. Milton ordered the evacuation of Apalachicola in March 1862 due to suspicion of interactions between the USN and

Cotton warehouses at Apalachicola in the 1800s. State Archives of Florida, Florida Memory Project.

Apalachicola today. Some of the larger brick buildings are old cotton warehouses. Author's photo.

sympathetic Unionists in the area. As was seen elsewhere in Florida, Navy personnel were supportive of these people, providing safe haven, supplies and other support. As the war progressed, the people increasingly turned to the U.S. Navy for support, rather than the Confederate government. On April 3, 1862, a large Union Navy landing party (well-armed) of eight boats from the steamer USS *Mercedita* and the gunboat USS *Sagamore* went ashore at Apalachicola. They were met by a crowd of citizens from the town, mostly women and children. Commander H. S. Stellwagen of the *Mercedita* addressed the crowd, telling them that they were not the "ruthless Hessians" that Confederate officials had portrayed them as, and they would not destroy any private property as long as the Navy men themselves were

Steam gunboat USS *Mercedita*. Naval History and Heritage Command.

not attacked or the private property was not used to aid and abet the southern war effort. Stellwagen gave them several older lighters and schooners that they could use to fish and harvest oysters from the bay for their needs. He burned the pilot boats *Cygnet* and *Mary Olivia* and the schooners *New Island*, *Floyd* and *Rose* (the latter loaded with cotton), due to their being more suitable for blockade running. Many in the crowd told him they were not "secesh" or sympathetic to the southern cause, but no one stepped forward to take the oath of allegiance to the Union.

As noted in Chapter 2, the Confederate Navy never had a real presence in Florida throughout the Civil War, mainly because of the lack of major ports and the decision by CSA leadership early in the war to not expend military resources defending the state. There was some Confederate Navy gunboat activity on the Apalachicola River, based out of the Port of Columbus, Georgia on the Chattahoochee River upstream. In early 1863, U.S. Navy Secretary Gideon Welles received reports of the construction of the Confederate gunboat CSS *Chattahoochee* in Saffold, Georgia, just over the border with Florida. The main purpose of this ship was to protect the industrial complex at Columbus, along with other important Confederate points on the

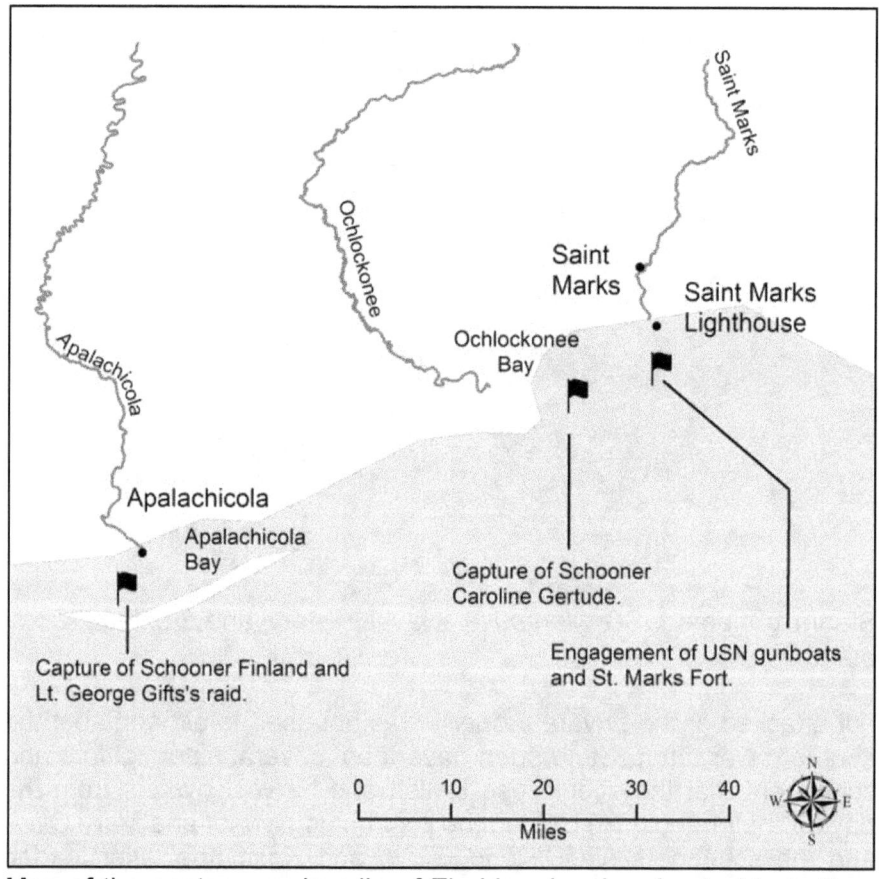

Map of the eastern panhandle of Florida, showing Apalachicola Bay, the St. Marks River area and naval events.

Chattahoochee/Apalachicola River system. Rumors also appeared to circulate that the ultimate purpose of this and other Confederate gunboats alleged to being constructed on the river was to break the blockade of Apalachicola, at the mouth of the river.

Welles sent orders to Rear Adm. Theodorus Bailey, commanding the East Gulf Blockading Squadron, to undertake reconnaissance up the Apalachicola River to ascertain the status of the Confederate gunboats on the river, with a view towards eventually conducting sorties to destroy or capture them. Bailey replied:

> Sir, I have the honor to acknowledge the receipt of your communication of the 10th of February, instructing me to examine into the subject of the reports which I forwarded from Lieutenant-Commander Crosman, and the practicability of an expedition for capturing or destroying the rebel gunboats on the Apalachicola, etc.
>
> I have made the enquiries and find that the river has a bar at the mouth, where it empties into St. George's Sound, with only 6 feet water on it at the highest spring tides; therefore the gunboats building on that river can not be formidable as ocean steamers. I think they are intended for river defense only, for the reason that the legislature of the State of Georgia, at its last session, passed a large appropriation of money to place obstructions in the rivers of that State, and from refugees and contrabands I learn that the rebels have fortified a bluff 80 miles from the mouth of the river and there obstructed the navigation by driving piles, etc. Above these obstructions the rebel gunboats are preparing and building.

He concluded by indicating that until shallow draft river gunboats from the Mississippi Squadron could be released to him, he could not attempt an expedition up the Apalachicola. That said, he maintained a flotilla of gunboats on patrol at the mouth of the river to confront and deter any Confederate Navy sorties.

In early May 1863, the CSS *Chattahoochee* was moored in the Apalachicola River near Chattahoochee, Florida. On May 9, Lt. George Gift of the *Chattahoochee* sent a dispatch to the ship's commanding officer, Lt. John J. Guthrie. Gift outlined a plan to take a large raiding party of rebel sailors and capture a Union Navy blockading vessel in Apalachicola Bay, based in part on the regular habits of its landing parties:

SIR: Conformably with your request, I beg to submit my views as to the feasibility of a descent upon the enemy at Apalachicola. I propose to take 60 men and a proper number of officers and proceed in the steamer Swan *to a point 6 miles from Apalachicola; there disembark at nightfall and march to a point near and in rear of that city. Arrived, I would use every precaution to prevent the fact of my presence becoming known. I would then send in two or three men, citizens of Apalachicola, apparently on leave. Their presence would be reported to Morris, of the enemy's* Port Royal, *on the first night, and on the second or third he would make his appearance as usual, with four boats' crews and a guard of marines – probably 60 men. His custom is to land and put his boat howitzer in position on shore and leave with it and his boats a guard of 10 or 15 men; with the remainder of his force he proceeds to search for his prey. My plan would be, first, to attack and overpower the party at the boats and gun, and then attack the remaining force when they return to the assistance of that party. Once in possession of the boats and the clothes of the prisoners, I would consider the capture of the* Port Royal *certain.*

The only doubt concerning the matter is getting Morris (i.e. a landing party from the Port Royal*) on shore, as I would have no doubt of the result of a battle as between the splendid crew of the* Chattahoochee *and a like number of Yankees surprised and taken at disadvantage.*

Gift was an ambitious and energetic officer. He later wrote Sec. Mallory with ideas for a naval attack on the Union in the Great Lakes. The plan he outlined above was not implemented until later in 1864.

On May 30, 1863, the CSS *Chattahoochee* was anchored near Blountstown, Florida, about 78 miles above the mouth of the Apalachicola River. Her commander, Lt. John Guthrie, had been informed that a Union Navy cutting out expedition had captured the blockade runner *Fashion* nearby, a schooner that had been loaded with cotton to run the blockade. Determined to avenge this, and demonstrate to the Union blockaders that it was the Confederate Navy which controlled the river, he had taken the *Chattahoochee* downriver hoping to get through a barrier of obstacles placed by the Confederates and recapture the *Fashion*. Not being able to do this, he ordered steam up to return to Columbus, Georgia. Something went terribly wrong during this procedure, and one or more of the ship's boilers exploded, killing 19 crewmen and injuring many others. The ship sank to the bottom of the river. Tragically, this was perhaps the only major effort by the C.S. Navy in Florida during the War, an effort that unfortunately ended in disaster.

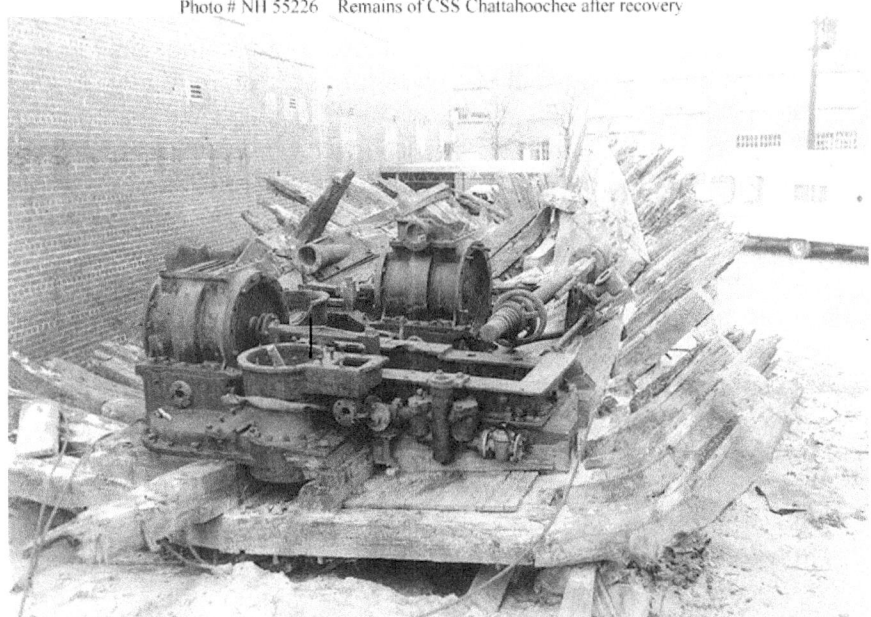

Remains of the CSS *Chattahoochee* salvaged from the Chattahoochee River in the 1960s. Naval History and Heritage Command.

Based on intelligence from escaped slaves, Lt. Commander A. F. Crosman of the USS *Somerset*, on blockade at the river mouth, reported the destruction of the *Chattahoochee* to Adm. Bailey in early June. The Confederates recovered all the ship's guns for use on shore batteries along the river, and eventually raised the ship itself, which was brought to Columbus for repair and refitting. She was deliberately destroyed at her moorings there in April 1865 to prevent capture by Union forces at the end of the war. Portions of the ship were recovered from the Chattahoochee River in the early 1960s. Those remains, and information about the ship, can be viewed today at the Port Columbus National Museum of Civil War Naval History in Columbus, Georgia.

In mid-1864, the ever-active Lt. George Gift, back in Florida from North Carolina, where he participated in a CSN raid on the Union gunboat USS *Underwriter*, decided to implement the plan he had proposed earlier to attack and capture a Union blockade warship off Apalachicola Bay. The C.S. Navy raiding party set out on May 3 from the CSS *Chattahoochee* in Georgia (now raised, repaired and under Gift's command), and making their way downriver in the steamer *Swan*, they picked up additional seamen and some Confederate Army troops. The CSN raiding force was assembled at Apalachicola by May 12 and set out that night to carry out their plan. Their target was the USS *Adela*, a fast, shallow draft side-wheel steamer built in Britain that was a captured rebel blockade runner. Unfortunately, as they set out in their boats, they were spotted by ship's boats from the gunboat USS *Somerset*. After landing a force of Union Army troops, supported by his seamen, to enter the town, Acting Volunteer Lt. W. Budd of the *Somerset* reported:

> *Taking two launches from this ship, I arrived in front of the place* (Apalachicola) *about the same time* (as the other Union force arrived in town), *and discovered a force of about 70 or 80 of the enemy attempting to embark in boats from the upper end of the wharves. The rapid approach of the first launch caused them to abandon that project and retreat through the town, which movement was hastened by a couple of shells from our howitzer.*

The U.S. Army troops entering the town thought the fleeing Confederates were part of their company and let them get away. Budd and his boats spotted Lt. Gift in the Bay escaping in one of his ship's boats with about 30 men and gave chase, but the speed of the rebel boat enabled them to outrun the USN boats. The Union forces captured six CSN ship's boats, a cache of small arms, ammunition, compasses, signal flags and other equipage left by the fleeing rebels. They also took four prisoners, three of whom were civilians of the town known to the USN personnel. They were sent to Key West as prisoners due to their providing assistance to the CSN forces in that effort.

St. Marks River and Adjacent Waters

The St. Marks River flows into Apalachee Bay, east of Apalachicola Bay and River. A lighthouse had been constructed at the river

U.S. Navy gunboat USS *Mohawk* off the St. Marks lighthouse. Confederate Navy gunboat CSS *Spray* is in the far background (to the left of the lighthouse tower). State Archives of Florida, Florida Memory Project.

mouth in 1830, but it was deactivated by the Confederates at some point in 1861. A wood and earthen fort with two 32-pdr and two 12-pdr guns was erected by the Confederate Army next to the lighthouse tower. On June 22, 1861, the steam gunboat USS *Mohawk* arrived off the river mouth. The ship's commander, Lieutenant J. H. Strong, sent a boat ashore under a flag of truce to give the fort's commander the declaration of the blockade establishment. On July 5, the *Mohawk* captured the sloop *George B. Sloap* trying to run the blockade (evidently the sloop's second try). The sloop had on board the wife, children and servants of Confederate Gen. Holland. Strong had these civilians rowed to the fort but kept the captain and crew of the ship as prisoners. He requested permission to send the sloop to Key West for adjudication, as he believed it was not worth the expense of sending it to a northern port.

In retaliation for an attack on a Union Navy watering party on the Aucilla River earlier that month (Chapter 6), on June 15, 1862, the gunboats USS *Tahoma* and USS *Somerset* hove to off the St. Marks lighthouse with its adjacent fort. At 1:50 in the afternoon, the *Tahoma* opened fire on the fort with her X (10)-inch Dahlgren gun and 20-pdr Parrott Rifle. Lt. J.C. Howell, commanding *Tahoma*, kept up the fire for just over a half-hour, then sent in a large landing party from both gunboats. The bluejackets and marines destroyed the battery and burned the rebel barracks present on the site.

Eight months later, on February 1, 1863, the steam gunboat USS *Stars and Stripes* was blockading the river mouth when she discovered a rebel encampment upriver. Her commander, Acting Master Charles L. Willcomb, ordered his guns to open fire on the camp. Willcomb reported:

> On the 1st instant I steamed in and came to inside of Long Bar, when I perceived a rebel encampment, which I shelled and caused the enemy to retreat to the town (St. Marks). What loss they sustained I am unable to state, as I could not see the effects of our shells.

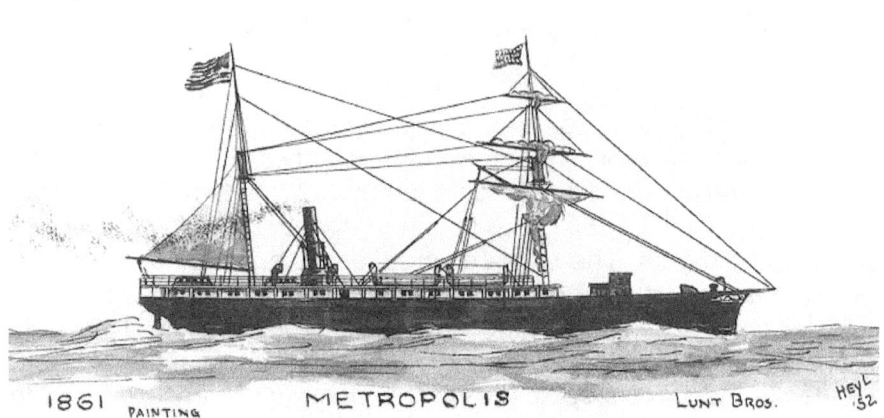

Steam gunboat USS *Stars and Stripes*. Artwork by Erik Heyl from Naval History and Heritage Command.

About two o'clock in the afternoon, Willcomb and crew spotted a small rebel steamer coming down the St. Marks River. The steamer stopped above Four Mile Point, "*apparently to reconnoiter,*" according to Willcomb's report. He ordered his sailors to fire on the steamer with the Parrott Rifle and saw,". . . *our shells bursting over and around them in such a manner as caused me to think she was hit. However, hit or not, they turned and steamed up again as far as they could beyond the fort.*" Based on maps of the lower St. Marks River from that time, the fort he references was a different structure from the one destroyed by the *Tahoma* and *Somerset* a year ago, next to the lighthouse at the river mouth. It was located upriver, protecting the Town of St. Marks and appears to be the "encampment" he referenced earlier. The pilot with the *Stars and Stripes* informed Willcomb that it would take a "high tide" to be able to take the gunboat up the river. Willcomb also noted in his report that he would largely stay just outside the bar at the river mouth, as at low tide he could not cross the bar either way (going in or out); he chose the lesser of "the two evils" he faced, to stay outside of the bar to keep his ship safer.

On July 12, 1863, Lt. Commander A.F. Crosman of the gunboat USS *Somerset* rendezvoused with the *Stars and Stripes* off the St. Marks River. Crosman informed Acting Master Willcomb that he intended to send a party of ship's boats up the river to take the rebel fort near St. Marks, and cut out the Confederate steamer *Spray* (which was probably the steamer Willcomb fired at in February). The "Official Records of the Navies" reports refer to the *Spray* simply as "a steamer," which seems to imply that it was a civilian vessel. However, historians George Buker and Frank Howard both refer to the ship as the C.S. Navy gunboat CSS *Spray*; a side-wheel steamer armed with three guns. She is also listed in the official "Dictionary of American Naval Fighting Ships" under the subsection "Confederate Forces Afloat" as the CSS *Spray*, which indicates she was armed with two guns and that she was a true Confederate Navy gunboat. That makes the *Spray* the only rebel gunboat entirely stationed in Florida during the war.

That night a landing party was dispatched up the St. Marks River, consisting of boats from both gunboats. Their objectives were to take the fort, capture the Confederate gunboat CSS *Spray* and take or destroy any other vessels they found. The landing party was spotted by rebel pickets, whereupon the Confederates opened fire with muskets and the guns of the fort. The Union boats withdrew and returned to their respective ships. The next day Crosman and Willcomb led a party in ships boats to sound out the deeper river channel, probably in hopes of bringing at least one of their gunboats up the river to engage the rebel fort and gunboat directly with their ships' big guns. They found a barge filled with stone sunk in the channel, which was an effective barrier to their gunboats. On July 15, Crosman and Willcomb snuck ashore at the St. Marks lighthouse and set fire to the wooden stairs inside the brick tower to prevent its use as a lookout station. They had orders to proceed to Ochlockonee Bay, and there they destroyed two large salt works, with an estimated value of $30,000, which perhaps made up somewhat for the failed expedition on the St. Marks River.

The evening of December 28, 1863, the *Stars and Stripes* discovered a schooner inside the mouth of the Ochlockonee River as they patrolled the coast. Acting Master Willcomb dispatched the first and second cutters, under the command of Acting Master Thomas Smith, with other officers and 20 men to capture the suspected blockade runner. At 2:30 AM on the morning of December 29, Acting Third Assistant Engineer William Hopkins came back alongside with thirteen prisoners from the schooner. She was the *Caroline Gertrude*, loaded with 69 bales of cotton and bound for Havana, Cuba. The ship had run aground at the river mouth on her way out.

Hopkins reported that Acting Master Smith believed that they could get the ship off the bar when the tide came in later that morning, but the ship was stuck fast and would not budge, even at high tide. Willcomb ordered most of the cotton to be off-loaded, but to use some of the bales to prepare "breastworks" on the schooner's deck to provide cover in case a party of rebel guerillas should happen by. As it turns out, that was clairvoyant thinking. Willcomb reported:

Capture of the blockade runner *Caroline Gertrude* by cutting out party from the USS *Stars and Stripes*. Note large cotton bales on deck providing cover. State Archives of Florida, Florida Memory Project.

> About this time, the enemy's cavalry made their appearance in large numbers and began a brisk fire, which was returned by our men from behind the cotton, the enemy

being behind trees and stumps, etc. The fire was kept up so lively that our men could not show their heads without being a target for at least 50 rifles. After a sharp engagement of two hours with them, and finding we could not save the vessel (an old affair) or any more of the cotton, at 3:30 set fire to her and she was totally destroyed, with balance of her cargo.

At 8 p.m. the boats returned to this vessel with 43 bales of cotton (2 being lost), which I now have on board and shall send to Key West by first opportunity, with all the papers found on board and the prisoners, 14 in all.

There were no casualties on the Union side, and Willcomb reported that the commander of the rebel forces was killed in the fire fight with the Confederate pickets on shore.

The gunboat USS *Tahoma* arrived off Goose Creek, just west of the St. Marks River mouth, on February 26, 1864. Her captain, Lt. Commander David B. Harmony, dispatched a landing party of three boats under the command of Acting Master Edmund C. Weeks, his Executive Officer. The boat expedition took advantage of a foggy evening to slip by Confederate pickets; their target was a salt works located in the marshes adjacent to the creek. The USN sailors were accompanied by a party of Florida refugees, one of whom acted as the pilot. They surrounded the salt works and captured the workers sleeping there. Slaves informed him about a nearby house with additional white workers, so Weeks sent a party of armed seamen there to capture those men so they could not warn a nearby Confederate cavalry unit when they heard the sounds of the destruction of the works. The salt works were demolished and Weeks returned to the *Tahoma* with his prisoners. The rebel pickets downstream were now alerted to the presence of the Union party and fired on them, but the sailors escaped with no injuries. In yet another gesture showing their sympathy for the southerners, Harmony paroled a Confederate officer with a leg amputated, two aged soldiers and the son of one of the latter. He kept the other prisoners, even though many were not in the Confederate Army, but Harmony reasoned that by making salt, they were aiding and abetting the enemy. You can view a photo of the remnants of one of the boilers from these salt works at http://www.panoramio.com/photo/8150700. The site is isolated in a salt marsh and not easily accessible.

Chapter 4. Actions in Northeast Florida 1862-1864

Retaking Ft. Clinch and Occupation of Fernandina

The Blockade Board had recommended capture of a southern port to serve as a coaling, repair and staging area for the South Atlantic Squadron. Initial consideration for the southeast coast included Bull Bay, St. Helena Sound, and Port Royal, all in South Carolina. Port Royal was selected as the preferred choice because of its excellent deep-water anchorage and ease of defense from a land attack. A joint Union Army/Navy expeditionary force captured this anchorage on November 7, 1861. After securing this main base of operations, attention looked south to the next target. The Port of Fernandina, Florida, was important due to its ability to handle all but the largest U.S. Navy ships in the entrance channel, its rail connections, and its proximity to the Bahamas (English territory and a key waypoint for blockade running). For a period of time (December 1861 to February 1862), the Union Navy was more occupied with blockading the Port of Savannah, Georgia. Eventually however, interest in taking Fernandina resumed and a detachment from the South Atlantic Squadron headed toward the coast of Florida.

The entrance to the St. Mary's River, which was the access to the Port of Fernandina, was guarded by Ft. Clinch. On March 3, 1862, U.S. Navy forces arrived off the mouth of the St. Mary's River (the Atlantic coast border between Georgia and Florida) and occupied Ft. Clinch. The fort, along with some well-constructed batteries in earthworks outside of the fort, was found abandoned, with a variety of artillery pieces in fine condition, along with powder and shot. The next day, the nearby town of Fernandina was occupied by Union forces. Ft. Clinch was turned over to U.S. Army troops a day or so later. Flag Officer Du Pont reported:

> . . . I learned from a contraband who had been picked up at sea by Commander Lanier, and from the neighboring residents on Cumberland Island, that the rebels had abandoned in haste the whole of the defenses of Fernandina and were even at that moment retreating from Amelia Island . . . . . on receiving this intelligence I detached the gunboats and armed steamers of light draft from the main line and, placing them under the command of Commander P. Drayton, of the steam sloop **Pawnee**, I

ordered him to push through the sound with the utmost speed, to save public and private property from threatened destruction . . .

Immediately on his entering the harbor, Commander Drayton sent Lieutenant White, of the **Ottawa**, *to hoist the flag on Fort Clinch, the first of the national forts on which the ensign of the Union has resumed its* (place).

We captured Port Royal, but Fernandina and Fort Clinch have been given to us.

Ft. Clinch after recapture by Union forces in March 1862. State Archives of Florida, Florida Memory Project.

During the occupation of Fernandina, one the weirdest events of the Civil War involving a U.S. Navy ship transpired, perhaps the only occurrence of an incident like this in the history of the U.S. Navy. As the USS *Ottawa* approached the town, they discovered a train departing with Confederate troops and refugees, one of whom was rumored to be former Florida U.S. Sen. David Levy Yulee. As the track ran along the Amelia River for a distance, the *Ottawa* went steaming up the river after the train, firing at it in the pursuit, which went for two miles. The gunboat fired on the train because her com-

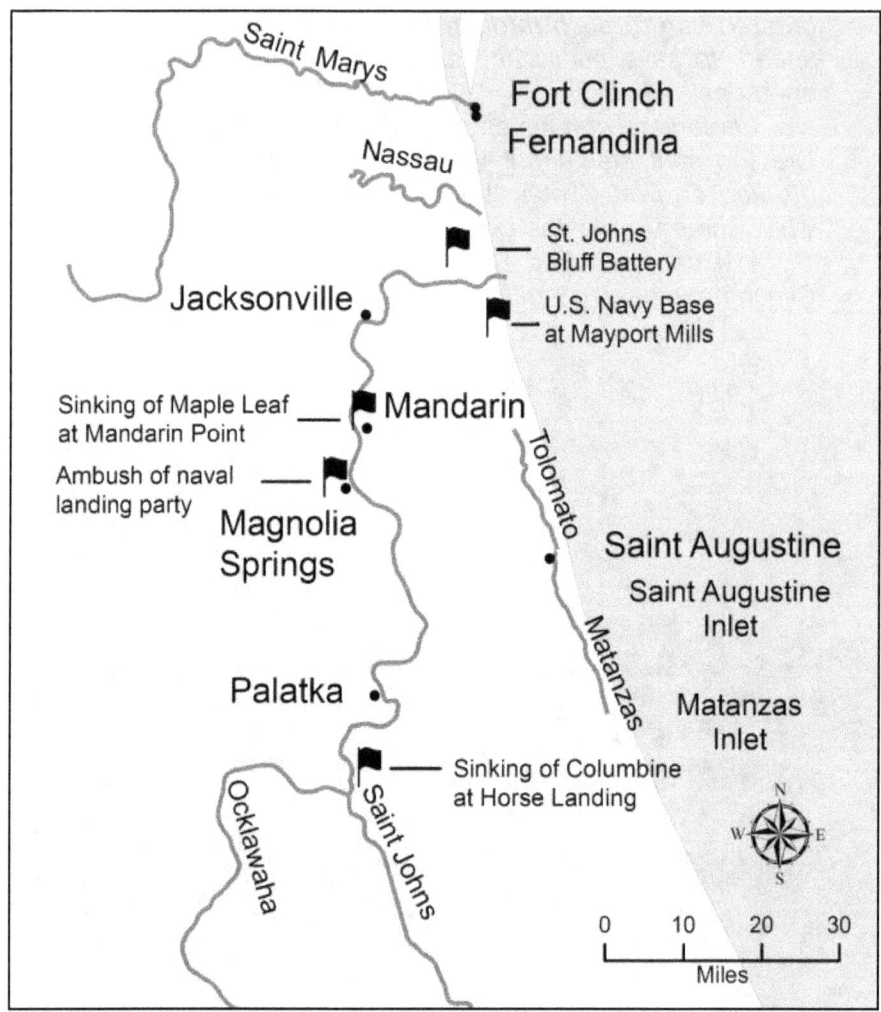

Map of northeast Florida, showing major cities, rivers and locations of naval actions.

mander believed that it was only carrying military personnel. One shell struck the last car on the train, killing two young men sitting on the pile of material stacked on the car. The car was detached and the train made its getaway.

As Union forces occupied Fernandina, Commander C.R.P. Rogers of the USS *Wabash* pushed up a small creek near the town in a ship's launch and captured the Confederate steamer *Darlington*, captained by Jacob Brock. Brock was a well-known steamboat captain on the St. Johns River prior to the war, who cast his lot with the Confederacy after Florida seceded. He initially refused commands to heave to, forcing the Union bluejackets to fire on the steamer, which eventually did stop and surrender. After boarding, the Union Navy officers were enraged, as there were a number of women and children aboard, who had been begging the captain to surrender as they were fired upon. Fortunately, no one was injured. Perhaps in retalia-

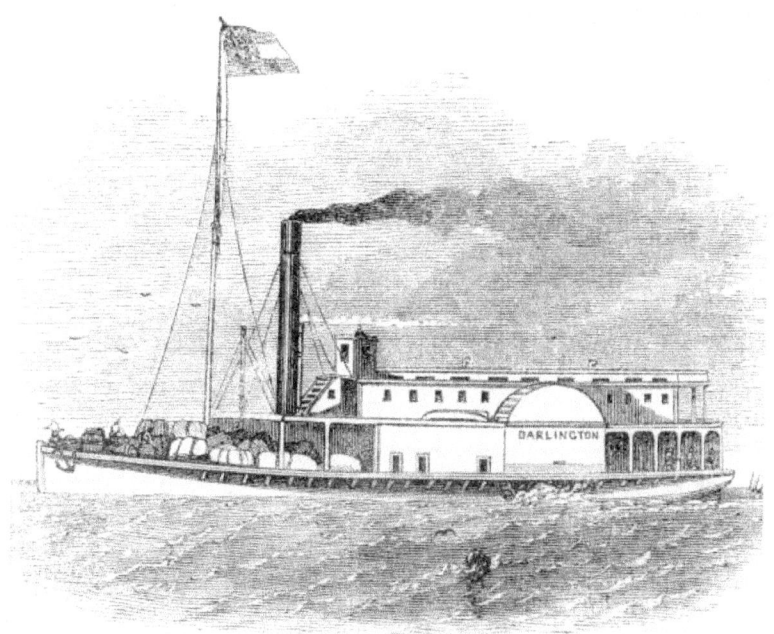

Confederate steamer CS *Darlington*, captured by Union forces during the occupation of Fernandina and renamed USS *Darlington*. State Archives of Florida, Florida Memory Project.

tion, Brock was arrested and sent to prison (even though he was not a member of the Confederate military), and his ship confiscated. In addition to the refugees, the steamer contained "military stores, and wagons, mules, forage, etc." and a surgeon in the Confederate Army. The captured steamer was converted into the gunboat USS *Darlington*, and was a participant in an expedition up the St. Johns River in October 1862.

Entering the St. Johns River and First Union Occupation of Jacksonville

Not long after taking Ft. Clinch and the Port of Fernandina on March 3, elements of the South Atlantic Blockading Squadron, along with transports carrying U.S. Army troops, arrived off the mouth of the St. Johns River on March 8, 1862. After reconnoitering the bar at the river mouth, and after repeated attempts to cross, Lt. Thomas H. Stevens of the *Ottawa* took the ship's helm himself, ordered "*full speed ahead*," and crossed the bar on March 11, along with the gunboats *Seneca*, *Pembina*, and *Ellen*. *Ottawa*, *Seneca*, and *Pembina* were all *Unadilla*-Class ("90-day") gunboats, and *Ellen* was a converted New York ferryboat. They captured Ft. Steele, a small earthen fortification strengthened with trunks of sabal palm ("palmetto" in some accounts), built by the Confederates in 1861 near the mouth of the river and armed with 6-8 guns (accounts differ). The rebels had abandoned the fort a few days earlier after sighting the arrival of the Union squadron off the river mouth.

On March 12, the first occupation of the City of Jacksonville occurred, as companies of the 4th New Hampshire Infantry Regiment were landed. Jacksonville had a fairly large population of pro-Union folks, who were overjoyed to see the Union occupation of the city. To their dismay, by the end of the month Army forces were ordered withdrawn from the city due to its "lack of military value." Officers on the Union Navy vessels were aghast at this action. In an effort to provide some assistance, the Navy established a permanent base of operations at Mayport Mills, near the mouth of the St. Johns River and about 6-7 miles downstream of Jacksonville.

U.S. Navy base at Mayport Mills, St. Johns River. State Archives of Florida, Florida Memory Project.

Palatka is a small town on the St. Johns River about 45 miles south of Jacksonville. The name of the town comes from the Seminole-Creek language, meaning "ferry" or "crossing," as the width of the river narrows substantially here, affording a place to cross more easily. For the citizens of Palatka, the morning of March 14, 1862 dawned uneventfully, that is until someone looked out on the river. Steaming upstream towards the city, belching coal smoke from its funnel, was an imposing black-hulled warship flying the stars and stripes of the Union. The minutes of the Session of the First Presbyterian Church of Palatka indicate, "*On March 14, 1862, the enemy entered Palatka . . .*" In his diary on this same date, Confederate sympathizer and blockade runner Richard J. Adams recorded, "*Federal Gunboat arrived at Palatka at 8½ A.M. – I took to the woods.*"

Sketch of the USS *Ottawa* on the St. Johns River. By the author.

The "Federal Gunboat" Capt. Adams referred to was the USS *Ottawa*, under the command of Lt. Thomas H. Stevens, a veteran of twenty five years of service in the U.S. Navy. The *Ottawa* was one of the new *Unadilla*-Class gunboats, nicknamed "90-day gunboats" because they were built so quickly. She was powered by both sail and a steam engine that drove a screw beneath the stern of the ship. She was also formidably armed, with an XI (11)-inch Dahlgren gun, mounted "in pivot," so it could fire in any direction, a 20-pdr rifled Parrott gun (also in pivot), and two 24-pdr smoothbore guns in broadside. The typical crew complement on these gunboats was about 80 officers, seamen, and marines (ranging from 65 to 100).

After supporting the landing of U.S. Army troops at Jacksonville on March 12, the next day Stevens and his ship made a probe up the St. Johns River to Palatka. In his March 17 report to Flag Officer Du Pont, he wrote:

> *Since my last communication I have made a reconnoissance* (sic) *as far as Palatka, and found no hostile demonstrations; on the contrary, the assurance I gave that we did not come to molest peaceable citizens has had a good effect . . .*

Stevens also found out that the famed racing schooner *America* was scuttled upriver in Dunn's Creek. The boat had been purchased by an English citizen, after winning what became known as the "America's Cup," and turned into a blockade runner. She had recently made a successful run into Jacksonville, but when the U.S. Navy arrived and sealed off the river her owner had the ship towed upriver and sunk. Navy personnel raised it a few days later, and she was

Schooner yacht *America*. State Archives of Florida, Florida Memory Project.

turned into a Union Navy blockading vessel. For the remainder of the war, USN gunboats were a constant presence as they patrolled the St. Johns River. Naval officers and men had numerous interactions with Florida citizens living along the river, assuring them that they were there to protect lives and property. Their efforts went a long way to fostering good will towards the Union in northeast Florida.

On March 10, 1862, the USS *Wabash* hove to off the mouth of St. Augustine Inlet, south of the St. Johns River mouth. *Wabash* was the flagship of the South Atlantic Blockading Squadron; she was one of the U.S. Navy's "capital ships" of the day, a huge steam-screw frigate, powered by square-rigged sail rig and steam engine. She packed a battery of 40 Dahlgren guns of various calibers. Shallow depths in the inlet and the harbor did not allow the *Wabash* to enter, and heavy weather that day restricted the use of ship's boats to cross the bar in the Inlet. The next day, March 11, Commander C.R.P. Rogers entered the inlet in a ship's boat with an unarmed landing party, arrived at the harbor, and accepted the surrender of Ft. Marion and the adjacent Town of St. Augustine. In the span of barely two weeks, the Union Navy and Army had secured a strong foothold in a big chunk of northeast Florida, securing fortifications, land, and secure harbors. This formed the basis for subsequent operations in this area of Florida.

The Union Navy, Union Loyalists, Confederates, and the Slave Population

The arrival of Union Navy warships on the St. Johns River galvanized the African American slave population along the river. As Dr. Dan Schafer noted in his writings, for the slaves, "freedom was as close as the river." Many slaves slipped away from their owners at night and tried to make their way to the Union gunboats to win their freedom. During the early months of 1862, when the Union Navy first occupied the river, one of the principal officers dealing with the "slave issue" was Navy Lieutenant J.W.A. Nicholson. He commanded the gunboat USS *Isaac Smith*. He had already been involved with rescuing and evacuating white residents of the area who were sympathetic to the Union cause, and who were being harassed or threatened by Confederate loyalists known as "regulators" or "guerillas." These were armed bands of militia, who believed it was their duty to enforce loyalty to the Confederate cause in the area, and/or take revenge on Union sympathizers.

Based on the number of escaped slaves he had retrieved and relocated, Nicholson believed that evacuation of slaves would be an exceptional drain on the southern economy in the region. In a June 17, 1862 dispatch, he reported to Adm. Du Pont:

> *I went up the river Saturday last, and remained over Sunday about 15 miles above Jacksonville; found everything quiet. Shortly after dark the contrabands* (escaped slaves) *commenced coming in, and when I started on my return, Monday morning, I had 43 on board, 12 of whom were children, besides 4 free blacks.*

He adds in a cryptic postscript:

> *The whole of the banks of the river is planted as far as one can see with corn. They say corn enough in Florida for all of the Southern rebel States. If we carry their* (slaves) *off they can not gather it; one consolation.*

African Americans, both slave and free, were terribly harassed during this time by the regulator and guerilla bands. Initially there was some confusion on the part of the U.S. Navy on how to deal with "the contraband question" (as slaves were considered "property," they were labeled "contraband" just as material goods would). Some officers abided by the Dred Scot Act, which required all escaped slaves to be returned to their masters. Policy seemed to evolve based on experience and personal bias. Some naval officers on the St. Johns only returned slaves to those owners willing to profess and swear loyalty to the Union, but confiscated or escaped slaves belonging to Confederate sympathizers were not returned. Some Confederate officers accused the U.S. Navy of encouraging slave defection, who in turn denied this in the strongest terms. Lt. Stevens wrote, "*. . . no encouragement or inducement has been offered on my part, or on the part of any officer or man under my command, to entice slaves away. My orders are stringent upon this subject and I know of no violation of them.*" By the middle of 1862, U.S. congressional action and Presidential decree mandated that all confiscated and escaped slaves were to be retained and afforded shelter, and that the decision of what to do with them would be made at the end of the war.

The Union Navy also had some not-so-pleasant encounters with Confederate sympathizers. One of these that captured much attention was a Mr. George Huston, who was believed to be one of the principal leaders of a gang of regulators threatening sympathetic Union folks, and whom was also believed to be the leader of the deadly ambush of USN forces at Mosquito Inlet in March (Chapter 5). He had also apparently lied about his loyalty to the Union to enable return of slaves to him. On June 8, Lieutenant Daniel Ammen sent Lieutenant John G. Sproston and a large group of 70 seamen to arrest Huston. When the USN detachment arrived at his house, Huston met them at the door, thoroughly armed, having been alerted to their coming. As Lt. Sproston stepped forward and demanded his surrender, Huston leveled his weapons on the naval officer and fired, killing him instantly. The naval landing party immediately returned fire, wounding Huston, who died eleven days later.

Towards the end of July, Lt. Nicholson was informed that a Unionist, a "Dr. Balsam," had been ordered to evacuate his property by a rebel guerilla band associated with the Broward family. He ordered the gunboat USS *Uncas* to proceed to the Broward plantation and fire on it. Arriving off the plantation, the *Uncas* lobbed a shell into the house, driving away a number of mounted militia. Nicholson proceeded there on July 31, 1862 with the *Isaac Smith* and heavily shelled the Broward house, mostly destroying it. A landing party went ashore and burned the remains of the house and all other structures on the plantation.

Actions with Confederate Battery at St. Johns Bluff

In the late summer of 1862, Confederate Brig. General Joseph Finegan, commander of the Department of Middle and Eastern Florida, began construction of an earthworks and battery of guns on St. Johns Bluff, on the south bank of the St. Johns River about four miles upriver from Mayport Mills, with the intent of restricting or halting U.S. Navy operations on the river. Possibly, he was acting under orders from Gen. Lee to attempt to secure the St. Johns and Apalachicola Rivers for continued use by the forces of the Confederacy. The work at St. Johns Bluff was completed September 9, 1862. Finegan also had a second battery of guns constructed at Yellow Bluff, on the north bank of the river about one mile upriver of St. Johns Bluff.

An escaped slave named Israel informed Acting Master W.D. Urann, of the USN gunboat *Patroon*, that the Confederates had constructed a battery at St. Johns Bluff. Evidently, the officers of the St. Johns River squadron had not yet learned to trust the information provided by these "contrabands," and were consequently skeptical of this intelligence. Urann relayed the contraband's report to Acting

Master Lemule G. Crane, of the steam gunboat USS *Uncas*, who decided to conduct his own reconnaissance up the river on September 10. Proceeding upstream, accompanied by the *Patroon*, Crane arrived off St. Johns Bluff at dusk. He had his crew set out a kedge anchor to enable his ship to bring its broadside to bear and fired nine shells into the bluff from the ship's 32-pdr guns and 20-pdr rifle. The rebels in the fortifications on the bluff did not return fire in an effort to keep their location unknown at that time.

The morning of September 11 dawned with a different experience. At daybreak, the rebel battery opened fire on the *Uncas*. Crane ordered the anchor cable slipped and cut loose the kedge anchor rigged the night before. The ship's guns had been run in for the purpose of swabbing the decks, and it evidently took some extra time to bring them into action. *Uncas* was hit five times, one shot actually penetrating the magazine, before the gunboat was able to begin maneuvering to avoid the fire from the battery and return fire. Crane signaled for the *Patroon* to come upriver to lend fire support. Due to the strong tidal currents in this portion of the river, it took an hour and

Harper's Weekly sketch of the Confederate battery at St. Johns Bluff. State Archives of Florida, Florida Memory Project.

a half for the *Patroon* to maneuver into position to bring its guns to bear on the bluff. *Uncas* and *Patroon* dueled with the battery for over four hours, expending 203 shell and 13 solid shot between the two ships. Crane reported that many of their shells exploded within and around the earthworks, and that they drove the rebels off for a short period of time.

Reports of the firing on the gunboats *Uncas* and *Patroon* by the battery on St. Johns Bluff outraged Flag Officer Du Pont. Until this attack, he had made it clear to the people of Jacksonville and the surrounding areas that the Navy would display no hostilities towards them if his ships were not "molested." He sent orders to Commander Charles Steedman to assemble a task force:

> *Since the withdrawal of our troops from Jacksonville, as you are aware, we have been simply maintaining an inside blockade of the river by a very small force near its mouth. I had it intimated in various ways to the citizens and authorities of Jacksonville that if the gunboats were molested from the banks of the river, or Union people maltreated and their property destroyed, that I would adopt retaliatory measures by destroying Jacksonville, etc.*
>
> *I have now to direct that you will proceed with the* **Paul Jones** *under your command to the St. John's* (sic) *River, taking with you, or to follow you, the* **Cimarron,** *Commander Woodhull; the* **E.B. Hale,** *Lieutenant Commanding Snell; and the* **Uncas,** *Acting Master Crane; the* **Patroon** *you will find in the river.*
>
> *Please make a thorough reconnoissance* (sic) *of the river as far as you deem it advisable and of service, going to Jacksonville and ascertaining by flag of truce what is meant by this attack upon our boats, and warning responsible persons of the consequences; destroy all the works on the banks which might be used or occupied by the rebels at any future time against us.*

Steedman's flotilla consisted of his side-wheel gunboat, the USS *Paul Jones*, plus the gunboats *Cimarron*, *Uncas*, *E.B. Hale*, and *Patroon*. Assembling at Mayport Mills on September 16, the task force headed upriver the morning of September 17, 1862. As the USN flotilla approached the battery, *Paul Jones* and *Cimarron* opened fire at a range of 2,000 yards with their big 100-pdr Parrott rifles. This fire appeared to have not much of an effect on the battery.

At a range of 1,600 yards, the rebel battery began to return fire. The gunboats *Uncas*, *Patroon*, and *Hale* misunderstood Steedman's orders to go into action in line ahead formation, and according to his after-action report their fire was "*of little, if any, service.*" It may be that instead of closing with the battery at a range sufficient to bring their lighter guns to bear, they followed *Paul Jones* and *Cimarron*, and consequently were mostly out of range. Historian Ed Bearss, in an article in the Florida Historical Quarterly, indicates that the smaller gunboats could not fire because the *Cimarron* and *Paul Jones* were in their line of fire. Steedman estimated that he was under fire from

Steam gunboat USS *Paul Jones*. Painting by W.R. May from Naval History and Heritage Command.

Steam gunboat USS *Cimarron*. Naval History and Heritage Command.

six or eight guns on the battery and in the adjacent woods. Exchange of fire between the gunboats and the battery continued for several hours. Both *Paul Jones* and *Cimarron* took hits from the battery.

As with the engagement on September 11, the gunboat fire was sufficient to drive the rebels away from the battery for a period of time. The Navy ships expended about half their ammunition in this engagement. Steedman gave orders to cease firing and retire down-river; he felt that to continue upriver to Jacksonville would allow the rebels to reoccupy the battery and put his ships at peril on the return trip downriver. C.S. Gen. Finegan reported that two of his men were killed and three wounded in the naval assault on the battery. Steedman sent the *Uncas* to Port Royal with his after action report to Du Pont, and to obtain fresh ammunition for his ships. The *Water Witch* was dispatched from Port Royal to Steedman, with orders to obtain fresh ammunition for the 100-pdr Parrott rifles from ships blockading the Georgia coast (as none was available at Port Royal for the *Uncas*). This was probably the largest naval action of the Civil War in Florida, in terms of the number of warships involved, but the failure to defeat the battery solely by naval means prompted Du Pont to realize that it would take a combined Army-Navy operation to silence the battery.

Planning for this operation began in the last weeks of September 1862. U.S. Gen. John M. Brannan was dispatched from Hilton Head, SC with a force of infantry, cavalry and light artillery, about 1,500 men in total. Du Pont directed Steedman to continue to harass the battery on St. Johns Bluff with "... *an occasional shot.*" Due to heavy weather, the departure of the expeditionary force was delayed until on or after September 23, when Du Pont authorized the expedition to proceed. The expedition departed on September 25. The gunboats *Paul Jones, Cimarron, Uncas, E.B. Hale* and *Water Witch* rendezvoused with the transports carrying Brannan's forces on October 1, 1862. They proceeded upriver to Pablo Creek and Mt. Pleasant Creek, where they began to land the Army troops, supported by U.S. Marines armed with Dahlgren 12-pdr boat howitzers. The force began to make their way towards the battery on St. Johns Bluff.

On October 2, concurrent with the developing assault on the St. Johns Bluff fortifications, Steedman ordered Commander Maxwell Woodhull of the gunboat *Cimarron*, accompanied by the *Water Witch* and *Uncas*, to conduct a reconnaissance of the Bluff. The battery commenced firing on the Union ships as they passed the mouth of Sisters Creek, the Union ships returning fire. The firing from the battery was well aimed, and the *Cimarron* encountered difficulties in maneuvering due to a combination of strong tidal currents, wind, and the poor handling characteristics of the ship, all of which made it difficult for Woodhull to bring his guns to bear on the battery. Amazingly, little damage was inflicted on the ships, even though many rebel shots landed close enough that the deck crews on the USN ships were doused with water. Both *Cimarron* and *Water Witch* ran aground for a period of time, during which they continued to receive fire from the battery. The fight continued for about an hour and a half, after which the three ships received a signal from Steedman to return downriver and help cover the troop landing. No casualties were suffered on any of the three Union ships, to Cdr. Woodhull's astonishment.

The infantry, cavalry, and artillery were all landed by October 3, and the Union force began to push its way west towards St. Johns Bluff. As they advanced, it was noticed that no flag was flying over the battery. Although this suggested the rebels had abandoned the works, Steedman was skeptical, since no flag had been observed flying the day before, when the battery fired on the *Cimarron*, *Water*

Sketch of the rebel battery at St. Johns Bluff after its capture by Union forces. From the Official Records of the Union and Confederate Navies.

Witch, and *Uncas*. In consultation with Gen. Brannan, Steedman dispatched the *Hale* and *Uncas* upriver to conduct another reconnaissance of the battery. Arriving off the battery, Acting Master Alfred T. Snell of the *Hale* ordered his guns to open fire, but received no return fire from the earthworks. He dispatched an armed shore party in the ship's gig to the battery, where they found that the rebel

View of the St. Johns River from the Ribault Monument park on St. Johns Bluff. This is close to the location of the Confederate battery and gives a perspective of the command this position had over movement on the river. Author's photo.

garrison had evacuated the works as the Union force pushed its way towards the Bluff. Union Navy forces raised the U.S. flag over the fortification on October 3, 1862. The battery upriver at Yellow Bluff, was also evacuated by Confederate forces on or about this date.

The St. Johns bluff battery consisted initially of six guns, supplemented with additional guns following the first engagement with the U.S. Navy on September 11. After its capture, the inventory of guns in the battery was: two 8" smoothbore, two 8" Columbiads, three 8" siege howitzers, and two rifled 4.6" guns, for a total of nine artillery pieces. Some field guns were also present, but those were taken by the rebels when they withdrew from the fortifications. The battery upriver at Yellow Bluff was armed with eight guns.

USN Patrol Activity on the St. Johns River, 1862

The conquest and occupation of the St. Johns Bluff battery opened the river to U.S. Navy forces to conduct expeditions up the St. Johns River. This they did, destroying or taking possession of every small boat, scow, or barge they could find in order to impede the ability of rebel troops and supplies to be ferried across the river.

Steam gunboat USS *Water Witch*. Library of Congress, Prints & Photographs Division, Harris & Ewing Collection, LC-H261-585.

In an October 4 expedition up the river by *Cimarron*, *Water Witch* and *Hale*, Cdr. Woodhull reported that 200-300 small vessels were destroyed. On the way up, the *Cimarron* continued to display poor handling, at one point steaming upriver stern first. Woodhull transferred his command to the *Water Witch* and continued the expedition up the river.

Arriving off Palatka on October 5, Woodhull reported that he met aboard *Water Witch* with former Florida Gov. Moseley and a unionist named Blood. Moseley reported that the rumor had been widely spread that it was the intent of the U.S. forces to arrest and execute or imprison every southern white man found. Woodhull sent Moseley back ashore with assurances that this was not at all the case, and that if the citizens of the region behaved peaceably, they had nothing to fear from the Union. During this meeting, a party of armed horsemen were spotted approaching the town by lookouts in the tops of the gunboats. Woodhull signaled for his boats to return to the ships and ordered Snell in the *Hale* to open fire on the mounted party. The fire was accurate and deadly, apparently killing three or four of the horsemen. The fire of the gunboat forced the mounted party to retreat back into the adjoining forests and swamps. Blood and his family and the families of black pilots who had assisted the Navy ships with navigation on the river were evacuated for their safety. Snell took the *Hale* to reconnoiter in the Orange Mills area (downstream of Palatka), then rejoined the squadron at Jacksonville.

In his report to the South Atlantic Squadron on December 3, 1862, Cdr. Woodhull described meeting in early October with a "Mr. Benedict," also referred to as Dr. Benedict, at his hotel/resort at Magnolia Springs (also called 'Magnolia'), on the St. Johns River. Woodhull described the hotel as:

> . . . a splendid three-story hotel, covering a large space of ground, surrounded by quite a number of beautiful cottage residences (part of the establishment). It all belongs to this Mr. Benedict, and has been a favorite winter resort in past years for invalids from the north. The property is very valuable and no expense has been spared, apparently, to make it an agreeable place of sojourn.

At this meeting, Mr. Benedict expressed his desire that the U.S. Navy assist in evacuating his son to the north to escape the Confederate conscription (Army draft). Several weeks afterward, Woodhull sent the steam gunboat USS *Uncas* on a patrol up the St. Johns River, and directed her commander, Acting Master W. M. Watson, to stop by the Magnolia Springs Hotel and meet with Benedict. Arriving off the hotel on November 28, Watson dispatched a shore party that met Benedict at the river end of the hotel's dock (described by Woodhull as "nearly 300 yards in length" – typical of docks on the river today. There is a very broad shoal of very shallow water along the shoreline of the river in much of this reach).

The dock and hotel at Magnolia Springs on the St. Johns River, probably after the war. State Archives of Florida, Florida Memory Project.

Benedict told the officer commanding the landing party that he no longer wished to send his son north, but he requested that they go ashore with him to receive some mail he wanted sent north. As the sailors, accompanied by the southern man, approached the shoreline end of the dock, Benedict suddenly darted beneath the structure. A group of Confederates in hiding (numbered at 50 men) opened fire on the landing party; it was a trap, and the Union bluejackets found themselves in an ambush. Amazingly, none were hit by the gunfire. They retreated back down the dock "in good order," under fire the entire time. When they were safely back in the ship's boat (and out of the line-of-fire), Watson had the *Uncas* open fire on the shore, pounding the attackers with shellfire. The landing party re-boarded the ship with no casualties.

After summarizing Capt. Watson's report, Woodhull wrote in his December 3 dispatch:

> *I extremely regret that at the time of the above occurrence, he* (Watson) *had not there and then destroyed everything within the range of his guns, which would have been the proper punishment for such barefaced treachery. I indeed was much inclined to proceed up myself next morning and retaliate with fire . . .*

However, Woodhull deferred on this and reported the incident to Rear Adm. Du Pont to await his orders. He was unsure whether Benedict participated in the ambush by his own initiative or if he was forced into doing so by the rebel partisans; up until this incident he was known as a supporter and friend of the Union. Du Pont told him to essentially "forgive and forget it."

USN Patrol Activity on the St. Johns River, 1863

The year 1863, the third year of the war, was a relatively quiet one for USN forces in northeast Florida. Navy gunboats and transports assisted with Army expeditions up the St. Mary's River and with the third occupation of Jacksonville in late March, along with the evacuation of Union troops from there after about a week. The *Uncas* was kept busy on various patrols up the St. Johns River during the month of January. A serious accident occurred on board her when the ship fired on some rebel pickets that may have represented a threat. The 20-pdr Parrot rifle exploded, severely wounding Acting Ensign W. L. Pavy.

In July 1863, command of the South Atlantic Blockading Squadron went to newly promoted Admiral John A. Dahlgren, replacing Adm. Du Pont. Sadly, Du Pont's failure to retake Ft. Sumter and close off the Port of Charleston in April that year with a huge force of ironclad vessels led to demand for his replacement, despite his otherwise competent command of the squadron. Commander Steedman in the USS *Paul Jones* continued occasional patrols up the St. Johns when he was not blockading off the Georgia coast. The steam gunboat *Norwich* was also on patrol in the river, and the USS *E.B. Hale* returned to Mayport Mills in mid-1863 to assist in patrols on the river. In November, another familiar gunboat, the USS *Ottawa,* returned to the St. Johns River patrol, now under the command of Lt. Commander S.L. Breese.

The Confederates Fight Back, 1864

One of the technologies used by the Confederacy to blunt the overwhelming superiority of the U.S. Navy was underwater mines, called "torpedoes" at the time. These were initially developed by America in the Revolutionary War and were used against the British Navy, but by the Civil War, technological advancements had vastly improved their effectiveness. By the early to mid 1800s, two types of detonation mechanisms existed, contact and electronic. In the former, the mine was detonated by contact with some type of trigger mechanism (either mechanical or chemical) which ignited a spark and exploded the power in the device. Electronically detonated mines were exploded by an electronic signal conveyed by a wire and triggered by a man hiding nearby on the shore. Mines were packed with from 50 lbs to a ton of black powder. Confederate naval officer and scientist Matthew Fontaine Maury was an ardent advocate for the use of torpedoes against the U.S. Navy and, with the Confederate Torpedo Bureau, designed a number of the devices used by the Confederacy during the war.

In March 1864, Confederate Gen. P.G.T. Beauregard, now in charge of coastal defenses in South Carolina, Georgia, and Florida, called for the mining of the St. Johns River in an effort to blunt the effectiveness of the U.S. Navy there. Part of his hope was to trap Union forces garrisoned in Palatka and Jacksonville and force them to withdraw due to the inability of the Navy to supply and reinforce them as a result of the torpedoes. Beauregard ordered Lt. Col. M. B. Harris to Florida, where he was aided by Capt. E. P. Bryan in the construction and emplacement of torpedoes in the river. Initial efforts building torpedoes were conducted at Camp Milton, west of Jacksonville. Union intelligence became aware of this activity and as a result the enterprise was moved to a location upriver on Doctors Lake.

Needless to say, the U.S. Navy was concerned about the mining of the St. Johns. Army patrols along the banks of the river were increased in an effort to intercept rebel parties placing mines, and sailors in small boats undertook patrols along the river to locate and destroy emplaced mines. The Confederates likewise beefed up their security, with scouts placed at strategic locations to warn the torpedo builders. They also had Lt. A. J. Steadman with the Confederate Signal Corps read and decipher messages conveyed between shore parties and Union gunboats.

An initial deployment of twelve torpedoes in the river was conducted on the morning of March 30 off Mandarin Point. In the evening that day, the Union transport *Maple Leaf* arrived at Jacksonville, discharging its load of soldiers and supplies. The ship took on board a group of cavalry and headed upstream to Palatka that night. After debarking this load, the ship was ordered to return to Jacksonville. She departed late on March 31. At 4:00 AM on April 1, the transport approached Mandarin Point on the trip downstream. She was guided by a free black pilot named Romeo Murray. All running lights were extinguished to avoid detection by Confederate snipers. Murray had the ship conned to the right of the channel to avoid a sand bar on the west bank. He later described hearing "*a loud noise*" beneath the hull of the ship and that the pilot house was "*lifted right up,*" throwing him

U.S. Army transport *Maple Leaf*. Source: Maple Leaf web site courtesy Dr. Keith V. Holland.

against the roof. The helmsman, Samuel D. Jones, reported hearing "*a heavy report*" and "*a cracking of timbers.*" The ship's Captain, H. W. Dale, was awakened by "*a tremendous crash and heavy report.*" Most of the bow end of the ship was wrecked by the explosion, and the ship quickly settled to the bottom of the river, with the upper works still exposed above-water. Four crewmen were killed by the explosion, and the 63 survivors took to the ship's boats and rowed to

Jacksonville. Dale reported the incident to his superiors and returned the next morning on the gunboat USS *Norwich*, finding the three Confederate prisoners they left the night before still marooned on the upper works of the ship that were out of water. Other than the tragic loss of the four crewmen and the ship, the major effect was the loss of a large amount of personal property belonging to the 112th New York Volunteers, the 169th New York Volunteers, and the 13th Indiana Regiments, leaving many with nothing more than the clothes on their persons. A Confederate Army detachment later rowed out to the ship and set fire to the exposed upper works.

The U.S. Navy responded by installing devices on its steamers and gunboats to deflect mines away from the ships' hulls. Small boat patrols on the river were stepped up to locate and disarm the torpedoes. Over the next week, 20 torpedoes were located and removed

Sketch showing sunken transports *Maple Leaf* and *General Hunter* on the St. Johns River. Alfred R. Waud drawing, Library of Congress, Prints & Photographs Division, Civil War Photographs, DRWG/US – Waud, no. 523 (A size).

from the river. The morning of April 16, a flotilla of three vessels (the Navy gunboat *Norwich* and the Army transports *General Hunter* and *Cosmopolitan*) passed Mandarin Point. Bryan and his men had placed additional mines in the river after the success against the *Maple Leaf*. The *Gen. Hunter* struck one of these and was damaged so severely that it sank in only a few minutes, with one life lost. This led to the withdrawal of Union forces from Palatka. The Union Army began a vigorous program of questioning local civilians in an attempt to locate and apprehend those building and placing the torpedoes.

The mining of the river upriver from Jacksonville apparently was effective in deterring Union Navy patrols along this stretch. Confederate attention then turned to the stretches of river downstream, between Jacksonville and the Navy's base at Mayport Mills. The morning of May 9, the transport *Boston* was steaming upriver from Mayport to Jacksonville, accompanied by the transport *Harriet A. Weed*, which was towing the schooner *Caswell*. Those traveling on the *Boston* looked astern at the *Weed* following them when they saw the ship lifted out of the water and shattered by the explosion of two torpedoes beneath its hull. In July 1864 a fourth transport, the *Alice Price*, was sunk by a torpedo off Cedar Creek, near Jacksonville.

It was a tremendous morale boost for southerners that a small group of determined defenders was neutralizing the effectiveness of the U.S. Navy on the St. Johns River, which minimized potential for Union Army raids into the interior. The resources for building torpedoes had been severely depleted by the middle of 1864, but Daniel Schafer has noted that some believed if resources were available, the Confederate defenders could have driven the Union out of Florida.

One of Florida's true military heroes during the war was Confederate Cavalry Capt. John Jackson Dickison. A native of Monroe County, Virginia (now West Virginia), Dickison moved to Florida in 1856. He owned a plantation at Orange Lake, north of present-day Ocala. In 1861, Dickison joined the Marion Dragoons as one of its officers. He later began forming another company of cavalry, but then switched it to an artillery company, the Marion Light Artillery. Eventually he left this group to form another cavalry company, Company H of the Second Florida Cavalry, C.S Army. Dickison's extensive knowledge of the terrain, back roads and trails throughout much of peninsular Florida made him one of the greatest threats to Union Army operations in Florida throughout the war. Time and again, he conducted guerilla operations which resulted in humiliating defeats for Union forces.

In April 1864, U.S. Gen. George H. Gordon received a report that a small garrison of his troops might be besieged by a Confederate force at their camp near Volusia, upstream of Lake George. On May 21, he departed Jacksonville with a company of 200 troops on the transport *Charles Houghton*, accompanied by the gunboat USS *Ottawa* and the armed tug USS *Columbine*. Gordon picked up additional troops at Picolata. They eventually found the garrison at Volusia to be secure and unharmed. Gordon appears to have headed north with his troops by land to return to Jacksonville. He dispatched the *Ottawa* and the transport back downriver to meet him there, the *Columbine* evidently remained in the Volusia area for another day.

On the way downriver, the *Ottawa* and the *Houghton* anchored near Palatka, and troops were disembarked on the east bank of the river. A rebel courier informed Dickison of the presence of the Union gunboat. In a remarkably emboldened and brash move, Dickison ordered Lt. Mortimer Bates to come with his two field pieces and had his second-in-command follow with the rest of his cavalry troopers. As night fell, Dickison placed his guns and troopers near Brown's Landing, about 200 yards away from where the *Ottawa* was anchored. For reasons unknown, the gunboat and the adjacent transport lit their running and deck lights, which made for perfect targets in the gathering dark. Dickison's men opened fire on the *Ottawa*, and although the formidable gunboat was eventually able to return fire, she was badly cut up by the rebel gunnery, with a number of sailors killed or injured. The damage to the gunboat necessitated a return to Jacksonville for repair and refitting.

Dickison was informed the next day of pending Union military activity by sympathetic civilians, who picked up this information from Union officers' "loose lips." One piece of information was that the armed tug *Columbine* was returning downriver from its foray to sup-

Ambush of the armed tug USS *Columbine* on the St. Johns River by Capt. J.J. Dickison and his cavalry. State Archives of Florida, Florida Memory Project.

port the garrison at Volusia. He placed his two field guns and a squad of sharpshooters in the swamps bordering the river at Horse Landing. The ambush party waited for several hours with no sign of the gunboat. The afternoon of May 23, a smudge of smoke could be seen upriver, and Dickison knew the *Columbine* was coming down. Interestingly, the gunboat's commander had been told to expect a potential ambush, and fired several shells into the woods at Horse Landing. Dickison's men took cover from this fire, and then re-manned their posts as the gunboat passed. At a range of about 60 yards, Dickison ordered his men to open fire. The first salvos were deadly; the ship's rudder chain was damaged, and the steam engine disabled. Most of the men in the ship's pilothouse were killed. The ship's commander, Acting Ensign Frank Sanborn, attempted a gallant defense of the now-crippled gunboat, but the casualties mounted and soon men began to jump overboard and flee the ship (many African American soldiers who feared for their lives). Sanborn eventually surrendered to Dickison. Fear that the *Ottawa* would return prompted Dickison to burn the *Columbine*, but before this a quantity of small arms, ammunition, and the ship's boats were taken, along with the two boat howitzers on the deck of the tug. This victory cemented Dickison's legendary reputation in Florida Civil War history, as this was the first known defeat of a Navy gunboat by a land-based Army force.

Despite these navy defeats, by the end of 1864 it was becoming evident that the Union would win the war. The U.S. Navy's blockade of the southern coast had been greatly solidified from its initial porous state and had tremendously crippled the southern economy. Powerful Union Armies were defeating the Confederates throughout the south, and it would only be a matter of time.

Chapter 5. Actions in South Florida 1862-1864

Mosquito Inlet/New Smyrna

As the war progressed, and the U.S. Navy blockade along the SE Atlantic Coast tightened around many of the main ports of entry in northeast Florida (Fernandina, Jacksonville and St. Augustine), Wynne and Crankshaw point out that blockade runners began to make use of more remote entry points in Florida to the south along the coast. Mosquito Inlet (now named Ponce de Leon Inlet), along the coast north of Cape Canaveral, became an important entrance point for runners. The inlet and Mosquito Lagoon were deep enough to accommodate larger steamers and schooners. The community of New Smyrna was located south of the Inlet along the Mosquito Lagoon. Runners would enter the inlet and dock at New Smyrna, or hide along the mangrove shoreline of the lagoon and offload their cargo. Wagons would transport the cargo overland to the St. Johns River, where it would be loaded on river steamers for transport to other offload points for transfer to railroad stations and further distribution. George Buker indicates that this was known as "running the inner blockade." Mosquito Inlet was the dividing point between the operating sectors of the South Atlantic Blockading Squadron (to the

Steamer docked at New Smyrna, probably after the war. State Archives of Florida, Florida Memory Project.

north) and the East Gulf Blockading Squadron (to the south), so ships of both squadrons participated in actions in this region.

In his report to Flag Officer Du Pont dated March 12, 1862, after the occupation of St. Augustine, Commander C.R.P. Rodgers (South Atlantic Squadron) wrote, "*I am led to believe that Mosquito Inlet, upon which Smyrna is situated, has been much used for the introduction of arms from the Bahamas.*" That very same day, the side-wheel gunboat USS *Keystone State* hove to off Mosquito Inlet. Commander W.E. LeRoy reported to Flag Officer Du Pont:

> *SIR: In obedience to your order of the 12th instant (March), I proceeded off Mosquito Inlet, anchoring the same afternoon, and on the following morning sent in a boat to make a reconnoissance (sic). We found that the channel had changed to the southward of the entrance marked by the buoy, the old one being entirely closed at low water. Owing to the sea on the bar, I did not deem it prudent to permit the boat to attempt to cross the bar, but on the morning of the 14th, I sent a boat inside, finding*

Steam gunboat USS *Keystone State*. Xanthus Smith sketch from Naval History and Heritage Command.

> *11 feet on the bar. I enclose accompanying a rough tracing of the position of the channel, with soundings, etc. The only vessel visible was a small schooner lying near*

the town of New Smyrna, where there were only 2 feet of water at low tide, and distant 2 or 3 miles from the bar. The boat's crew landed on one of the points, but nothing of interest was discovered. On the evening of the 16th, the Penguin *arrived, and, in obedience to the verbal order brought me by Lieutenant Commanding Budd, I left this morning at 9 o'clock, having delayed the night to enable me to supply the* Penguin *with coal to the amount of 20 tons.*

On March 19, 1862, Flag Officer S.F. Du Pont, of the South Atlantic Squadron, sent orders via the gunboat USS *Henry Andrew* to Acting Lieutenant T.A. Budd of the USS *Penguin*. The *Henry Andrew* was a sailing brig converted to a screw steamer and the *Penguin* was a screw steamer. Both were well-armed with 32-pdr smoothbores and rifles and howitzers. Between March 19-21, the *Henry Andrew* rendezvoused with the *Penguin*. Du Pont's orders were for the two gunboats to head to Mosquito Inlet and conduct a reconnaissance of the inlet and nearby town of New Smyrna. Their specific tasks were to reconnoiter and buoy the channel leading into the inlet (in order to allow one of the gunboats to enter and establish the blockade there), and capture or destroy the Confederate steamer *Caroline* (also named *Kate*) if it was present. Du Pont also informed Budd of the possible presence of a load of cut live oak timber, which he was ordered to take possession of and hold until shallow draft scows could be sent to retrieve it.

The evening of March 21, a party of four or five ship's boats were disembarked from the *Andrew* and *Penguin*, with about 43 men, and under the command of Lt. Budd and Acting Master Mather, commander of the *Andrew*. The landing party penetrated 15-18 miles up the Mosquito Lagoon, then decided to head back downriver. The boats were in sight of the *Henry Andrew*, when Budd and Mather noticed an earthworks on the nearby shore. By this time the boats appear to have become widely spaced out, and Budd and Mather, together in the same boat, decided to recon the earthworks. They appeared abandoned and were surrounded by dense forest and underbrush. As the boat slid ashore, rebels in concealment in the forest opened fire on the landing party. Lt. Budd and Master Mather were killed immediately, along with three of the five other sailors in the boat. The remaining two seamen were injured by the musket fire and took cover.

The remaining boats in the landing force approached the shore to lend aid and were also fired upon, the Confederate musketry cutting up the boats and their occupants badly. The trailing Union boat had a Dahlgren boat howitzer aboard, but it evidently was not set up to fire. The sailors in the remaining boats landed and took cover for the rest of the day. Under cover of darkness on March 22, Acting Masters Mate McIntosh led some men back to the beached ship's boats, took all the small arms, ammunition and flags, recovered the body of one of his dead shipmates, and had the howitzer thrown into the bay. He then returned to the *Henry Andrew*.

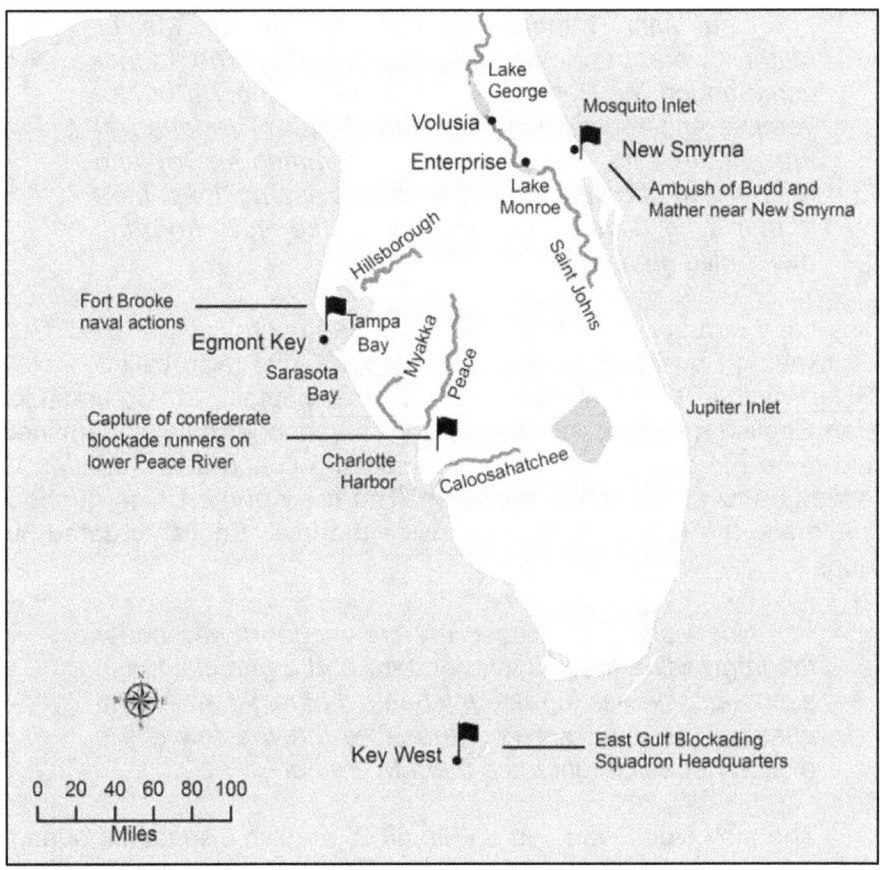

Map of the southern Florida peninsula, showing bays, rivers, towns and naval events.

Du Pont arrived off the inlet in the flagship USS *Wabash* sometime on March 22 and received a report of the incident from the *Penguin's* Executive Officer. He ordered his flag captain, Commander Rogers, to dispatch ship's boats to support the *Henry Andrew*. It appears that the gunboat, accompanied by the *Wabash* ship's boats, was able to enter the inlet and anchor near the site of the ambush. Under cover of the ship's guns, a landing party went ashore and met Capt. Bird of the Confederate Army, under his flag of truce. The Confederate officer turned over the bodies of Lt. Budd and Master Mather, along with papers and personal effects, and behaved with great courtesy towards the Union Navy men. Du Pont later wrote in his report:

> *Lieutenant Commanding Budd and Acting Master Mather were brave and devoted officers. The former commanded the* Penguin *in the action of the 7th of November and received my commendation. The latter, in the prime of life, was a man of uncommon energy and daring, and had no superior, probably, among the patriotic men who have been appointed in the Navy from the mercantile marine.*

On February 28, 1863, the USS *Sagamore*, of the East Gulf Blockading Squadron, hove to off Mosquito Inlet (also called "Indian River Inlet" in some officers' reports). Her captain, Lt. Commander Earl English, received intelligence that a schooner (later determined to be the *Florence Nightingale*) was loading cotton and preparing to attempt a run through the blockade. The crew of the Union gunboat could see the schooner moored inside the inlet. English ordered his guns to open fire:

> *Not wishing to expose my crew when I was under the impression they* (Confederates) *had a gun planted in such a position as to rake any boats that might attempt to pass up the narrow river, I therefore threw a few shells over in hopes I might force them to fire her.*

The ploy didn't work, so on March 2, English dispatched a landing party under the command of Acting Master J.A. Slamm. The party consisted of the ship's launch, first and second cutter, and gig with 41 total officers and men. As the landing party approached the schooner, Slamm observed a small group run aboard her and set torches. By the time the Union boats drew near, the schooner was catching fire. Slamm dispatched the men in the two cutters to board the ship, attempt to extinguish the flames, and bring it out to the gunboat as a prize. Slamm had a boat howitzer mounted on the bow of his launch, and he fired shell and canister into the adjacent shore area as covering fire. Despite this, rebels in concealment opened fire on the men boarding the schooner. The Union men returned fire, but were unable to extinguish the spreading flames, plus the schooner was hardaground due to the falling tide. Thinking that his basic objective was met (to take or destroy the schooner), Slamm ordered a general withdrawal. Seaman Hugh Maguire was killed in this engagement, along with several seamen wounded (three were subsequently described as "severely wounded" by the ship's surgeon).

In his report to Lt. Cdr. English, Slamm noted he observed large caches of cotton piled onshore, but was unable to do anything against this contraband due to the defense put up by the Confederate protectors. In accordance with the "fortunes of war," the Confederates were evidently able to extinguish the fire on the *Florence Nightingale* after the Union forces withdrew. The blockade runner then made a run for it and was captured by the steam gunboat USS *Octorara*. To the surprise of Lt. Commander English and his crew, the *Florence Nightingale* came sailing into the harbor at East Gulf Squadron Headquarters at Key West on March 17, 1863 as a prize to that fortunate gunboat.

The Mosquito Inlet and blockade running continued to torment the Union blockaders. In a major effort to put an end to it, on July 28, 1863 a squadron of U.S. Navy gunboats, under the command of Lt. Commander English, arrived off New Smyrna: USS *Sagamore* (*Unadilla*-Class gunboat), *Para* (mortar schooner), *Beauregard* (schooner), and *Oleander* (steamer). The *Oleander* took *Beauregard* in tow and they hove to inside the inlet and commenced shelling the town from offshore. English dispatched a large landing party of bluejackets and marines in ship's boats into the harbor. They captured one sloop loaded with cotton, a schooner without cargo, and caused the rebels to set fire to other sloops in the harbor, some loaded with cotton. The rebels also burned the large quantities of cotton stockpiled on shore. The landing party then went ashore, headed into the town, and destroyed and burned numerous structures (shops and homes).

The *Sagamore* continued to patrol the area, and on August 8, 1863, she "hit the jackpot." All on the same day, the ship and crew captured the English sloop *Clara Louisa* in the morning, and in the afternoon the English schooners *Southern Rights* and *Shot*, and the American schooner *Ann*. Evidently at least some of these were bound for Jupiter Inlet, to the south, so English recommended stationing a blockade vessel off that entrance. Despite this energetic Union blockading activity, Wynne and Crankshaw note that the Mosquito Inlet continued to be used by blockade runners through much of the rest of the war, and was never really entirely "closed down."

The Southern St. Johns River

A cutting out expedition set out on October 6, 1862 to capture the Confederate steamer *Gov. Milton*, and another steamer on the St. Johns River upstream of Lake George. It was known that the *Milton* was responsible for ferrying rebel troops and guns to the fortifications on St. Johns Bluff (Chapter 4), and that it was also important in conveying supplies run through the blockade to Confederate forces. Under the command of Lt. Commander E. P. Williams, the captured Confederate steamer *Darlington* (rechristened a U.S. ship with the same name, and armed with one or two 24-pdr boat howitzers) steamed upriver, accompanied by the gunboat *E. B. Hale*. At the entrance to Lake George, shallow depths wouldn't allow *Hale* to proceed further, so the *Darlington* continued upriver through Lake

Captured Confederate steamer CS *Milton*. Note Union "jack" flying over the Confederate flag at the stern of the vessel; a sign of a capture in naval tradition. State Archives of Florida, Florida Memory Project.

George, leaving the *Hale* to patrol the entrance to the Ocklawaha River, nearby.

At Hawkinsville, 168 miles upstream of Jacksonville (near present-day Deland), Williams and his men found indications that the *Milton* was in the area. Taking a party of sailors and soldiers of the 47th Pennsylvania Volunteer Regiment, Williams proceeded up a small creek in ship's boats and found the *Milton*, manned by only two engineers. They took possession of the steamer and reconnoitered up the creek further in search of the other steamer, then out into the St. Johns River as far up as Lake Beresford. When the steamboats could go no further due to shallow river depths, running low on fuel and rations, and deep in rebel-held territory, Williams decided to proceed back downriver to the squadron. Along the way up and back down river, numerous small vessels and other rebel property was destroyed or confiscated by the Union expedition.

On March 14, 1864, the armed tug USS *Columbine*, Acting Ensign F. W. Sanborn commanding, departed Palatka after supporting the landing of U.S. Army troops there. Sanborn and his ship proceeded upriver through Lake George and anchored for the night just south of the lake after crossing Volusia Bar. Earlier, on March 12, they had captured the Confederate steamer *General Sumter* in Lake George, and Sanborn had sent her upriver with a crew of officers and seamen from the USS *Pawnee* to look for other prizes. The *Columbine* got underway the morning of March 15 and continued south into Lake Monroe. Near the town of Enterprise, Sanborn saw two steamers heading across the lake towards his gunboat; it was the *Sumter* and the *Hattie* (also called the *Hattie Brock*, one of Jacob Brock's other steamers), the latter having been captured by the *Sumter*. He sent a prize crew aboard the *Hattie* and dispatched the steamer downriver. He then received some intelligence of the location of a sugar refinery about two miles from Enterprise. He sent one of his officers with seven soldiers from the 48th New York Regiment in the ship's launch on a shore party raid. They found the works and destroyed much of them, and impressed the slaves present, along with some cattle and wagons. These they transported to the shore, where they were loaded on *Sumter*. The withdrawal was somewhat hasty as the landing party was apprised of the approach of 30-40 partisan guerilas. *Columbine* took the *Sumter* in tow and headed downriver. They found the *Hattie* "ashore unmanageable," about ten miles downstream, although Sanborn does not indicate why. He also took the *Hattie* in tow and the flotilla continued downriver.

The morning of March 17, they arrived at Volusia, just south of the entrance to Lake George. They found a cotton gin and corn mill, which they took possession of and loaded aboard *Hattie*. A boiler powering these was destroyed. That afternoon they attempted to enter Lake George. *Columbine* grounded on the Volusia Bar at the south end of the big lake. *Hattie* also grounded, but the *Sumter* had a shallow-enough draft to slide over the bar. Sanborn off-loaded his guns, ammunition, and stores to try to lighten the *Columbine*. He and his crew struggled to free the gunboat and the captured steamer. He sent the *Sumter* back up to Volusia to load up on wood to fire all the

Sketch of a small rebel steamer captured by Union forces on the St. Johns River. Alfred R. Waud drawing, Library of Congress, Prints & Photographs Division, Civil War Photographs, DRWG/US – Waud, no. 341 (A size).

ships' boilers, as they were running low. His crew was able to free the *Hattie*, and the morning of March 19, after considerable effort, they were able to free *Columbine*. They continued the journey downriver, along the way capturing components of a turpentine still near Welaka. They arrived back at Palatka sometime around March 19 or 20 (Sanborn's March 20 report in the Official Records is vague on this). The expedition brought down with them 130 bales of captured cotton, 13½ barrels of turpentine, 25 barrels of rosin, and railroad iron. Barely a couple months later, the *Columbine* was destroyed at Horse Landing in an ambush by Confederate cavalry under Capt. John J. Dickison (Chapter 4).

The Indian River Lagoon/Southeast Florida

The southeast coast of Florida, from Cape Canaveral south to Cape Florida and Biscayne Bay, was exceptionally remote during the Civil War (the cities of West Palm Beach and Ft. Lauderdale did not even exist yet, and Miami was a small village). The U.S. census of 1860 showed less than 200 families living along this part of the peninsula, from current-day Titusville to Miami. Confederate sympathizers had extinguished most of the lighthouses along this stretch, making navigation difficult. Running parallel to the coast inside of the coastal barrier islands, the Indian River Lagoon tempted blockade runners, due to its remoteness, shallow depths, and proximity to the southern St. Johns River, which was used by rebel steamboats to transport contraband goods to rail points for shipment north to other areas of the Confederacy.

The Lagoon had a northern entrance at Haulover Canal and a southern entrance at Jupiter Inlet. The latter was deeper and wider, offering easier access, and was quickly adopted by blockade runners for use. Lack of mention of the Lagoon in the "Official Records of the Navies" may indicate that it wasn't until the latter part of 1862 that the U.S. Navy was able to devote ships to blockade there. In the latter part of 1862, the USS *Sagamore* (Lt. Commander Earl English) took up station off Jupiter Inlet. *Sagamore* had served earlier that year off Apalachicola, and subsequently saw blockade service off Tampa Bay, Cedar Key, and southwest Florida. She arrived off Jupiter Inlet after participating in blockade and raiding activities off Mosquito Inlet (see earlier this chapter). On December 5, 1862, the *Sagamore* captured and burned two sloops in Jupiter Inlet. Five days later they captured the English schooner *Alicia* up the Indian River, loaded with cotton and ready for a try at running the blockade. English sent the prize to Key West for adjudication.

In early January 1863, Assistant Surgeon Walter K. Scofield of the *Sagamore* recorded in his diary:

> *Jan 5 1863 . . . Jupiter Inlet . . . Captured the sloop 'Avenger' inside loaded with gin dry goods soap and coffee. Gin received on board for safe keeping . . ." "Jan 8'63. . . . Captured the prize sloop 'Julia' six miles north of Jupiter Inlet – Captain of her one Cummings or Matthews half drunk – Insulting language to our captain by this secessionist – He formerly owned land at Jupiter with one Smith but was ruined by a freshet forming new*

inlet and thus flooding his corn and potatoes six months ago. . .

Both prizes were sent to Key West. The morning of January 28, 1863, a boat from *Sagamore* took the sloop *"Elisabeth"* or *"Eliza"*, loaded with gin, coffee, flour and salt. The ship's captain evidently escaped the night before when he spotted the approach of the Union warship. Dr. Scofield relates, *"Boat sent after him to capture the captain – Sweeden a man we had caught once before while attempting to run the blockade. He made a boast at that time saying the 'Sagamore' never would catch him again."*

On December 22, 1862, Adm. Bailey of the East Gulf Squadron dispatched the U.S. Bark *Gem of the Sea* to Jupiter Inlet to assist the *Sagamore* in maintaining the blockade there. On January 1, 1863, Acting Volunteer Lieutenant I.B. Baxter, commanding, reported to squadron command that his boats captured the Bahamian sloop *Ann* on December 30, 1862 in the Indian River, six miles up from Jupiter Inlet. She had evidently run the blockade just the day before and contained salt, coffee, four gross of matches (576 boxes) and assorted dry goods. The condition of the sloop was so poor that Baxter didn't think her worth sending to Key West as a prize, so he ordered the ship's cargo to be confiscated and the runner burned.

The morning of April 8, 1863, Baxter and his ship were lying two miles off Mosquito Inlet in fog, as the fog lifted one of the lookouts hailed the deck, calling attention to a schooner to the northeast and heading south. The bark fired a warning shot, which was ignored. Baxter then ordered the gunboat to make sail and they gave chase for a period of time, until again they ran into a fog bank. A tense period no doubt passed, as the blockaders probably thought they had lost the prize. But things cleared again about 3 PM, and they spied the schooner heading back north and making for Jupiter Inlet. The depths at this time were too shallow for the bark to give chase, so ship's boats were debarked and they overhauled and captured the schooner, which was the *Maggie Fulton*, an English schooner running out of the Bahamas. She was carrying salt and "general merchandise." Baxter designated a prize crew and sent his capture to Key West with the crew made prisoner.

Henry A. Crane lived in Tampa at the outbreak of the Civil War, where he had dwelt since 1852. While his son left to join the Confederate Army, Crane remained a loyal Unionist. In the latter part of 1862, Crane decided to leave his family to join up with the Union cause. He made his way south and then over to the east coast, where he hailed a Union gunboat at Mosquito Inlet. He brought with him several other men, including one Mr. James Armour, who had a detailed knowledge of the Indian River Lagoon from his years working there as a commercial fisherman. The gunboat brought the refugees to Adm. Bailey at Key West for a discussion.

Bailey accepted Crane's and his men offer of service. He decided to give them acting positions on the USS *Sagamore* to provide the protection of being designated "enemy combatants" were they to be captured by the rebels. To be doing this work as civilians would mean they would be accused and convicted as spies and traitors and would be summarily executed. Bailey issued orders to Lt. Commander English of the *Sagamore*:

> *Sir: You will receive upon the* Sagamore, *as supernumerary volunteers, for pay and rations, seven refugees from the Indian River. Proceed to the mouth of that river and allow them to leave you in the night in a boat, which they will take with them, on an enterprise proposed by them for the capture of a rebel steamer.*
>
> *Remain in the vicinity or at Jupiter Inlet sufficient time to satisfy you that they have succeeded or failed, say a week or 10 days, and then return and report to me. Should the party not have returned before your leaving, you will give directions to the commander of the bark* Gem of the Sea *to look out for them, and in case they return to take them on board. Be vigilant in making captures of enemy's vessels and illegal traders breaking blockade.*

Crane was named Acting Volunteer Master's Mate, one of his men a First-class Fireman, and the remainder Landsmen. They joined the *Sagamore* in early January and began their expedition up the Indian River. Crane reported to Lt. Commander English that:

January 3-4, 1863 – captured the schooner *Pride* from Nassau, with her crew. Loaded with salt, which was destroyed. The prize and the boat expedition returned to Jupiter Inlet to find the *Gem of the Sea*, where they turned over their prize and left one of the refugees who had fallen very ill.

January 7 – accompanied by a boat crew from the *Gem of the Sea*, the refugees returned up the Indian River and captured a "small boat," along with camp supplies and provisions and two southerners believed to be serving as spies/lookouts, which they made prisoners.

January 9 – with the same group, captured the Bahamian schooner *Flying Cloud* (empty and unmanned) at the St. Lucie River and burned her.

January 16 – found a cache of 45 sacks of salt near Jupiter, which they destroyed.

Photo of the Jupiter Narrows area, Indian River Lagoon. State Archives of Florida, Florida Memory Project.

January 17 – captured a small boat and two men near the St. Lucie River.

January 18 – found a stash of four bales of cotton in the St. Lucie River.

February 2 – found a cache of salt near Jupiter and destroyed it. Sent a party of five men on February 3 on an expedition to Jupiter Narrows, where they found four bales of cotton, returning with them a couple days later.

February 7 – his ill man recovered and returned to his group, Crane and his men found salt, barrels of sperm oil, and assorted dry goods near Jupiter Inlet.

However, he never did find the Confederate steamer that was the original object of his raid. His original orders were to proceed up the Indian River, then over to the St. Johns River to find and intercept the steamer, then bring her downriver to the Navy base at Mayport Mills, or destroy it if this was impossible. But his exploits were evidently intrepid enough to satisfy Lt. Commander English and Adm. Bailey. On February 12, he and his men found a hidden stash with many "articles" from the nearby Jupiter Inlet lighthouse, plus salt, tools, etc. The "barrels of sperm oil" they had found earlier were probably the fuel used to fire the lighthouse's lantern.

On February 20, he and his men set out again, moving at night to prevent detection. Above the St. Sebastian River, they observed a rebel schooner moving downriver. Crane believed the number and attitudes of the men on the deck of the schooner suggested they were ". . . *designing to act on the offensive*," maybe attack a smaller boat party of Union sailors, or harass Union sympathizers. Crane let

Lighthouse at Jupiter Inlet. State Archives of Florida, Florida Memory Project.

the schooner run by him, then surreptitiously followed until nightfall, whereupon he and his men made a dash to board and capture her. She was the Bahamian schooner *Charm*, and carried no cargo. Taking possession of the schooner, Crane continued downriver and spotted a sloop at anchor ahead. They ran down and captured her, unmanned and loaded with cotton (evidently left there for someone to pick up; possibly some of the men in the schooner?). Crane divided his men among the two captured ships and continued downstream to Jupiter Inlet, arriving there on February 27. The next day he found the *Gem of the Sea* and turned over his prizes and prisoners.

Crane accomplished a number of other feats working with the Union Navy. He was eventually sent with the *Sagamore* over to the Gulf coast, where he was a participant in the joint boat expedition with the USS *Fort Henry* to attack the harbor at Bayport, and he also guided the crews of the USS *Tahoma* and *Adela* in their expedition tocut out the *Scottish Chief* and *Kate Dale* on the Hillsborough River in Tampa Bay (Chapter 6). In between these two exploits, he spent time in the Charlotte Harbor area making raids inland on Confederate supplies and property. In all his exploits, he came in contact with many Union sympathizers, whom he helped to link up with Union forces, particularly the U.S. Navy.

Southwest Florida/Charlotte Harbor

Almost a mirror image to the southeast Florida coast, the coast of southwest Florida from the Keys up to Tampa Bay was the very definition of "remote." Small fishing villages appear to have been established near present-day Ft. Myers, at Punta Gorda, up the Peace River (called "Peace Creek" in reports from the time), and small camps and individual settlements on some of the ancient Calusa Indian shell middens scattered throughout Pine Island Sound and the adjacent Ten Thousand Islands area to the south. The largest water body along this coast was the estuarine bay known as Charlotte Harbor. Two rivers, the Peace and the Myakka, drained into this bay from the interior of the state. The Caloosahatchee River drained into San Carlos Bay just south of the mouth of Charlotte Harbor.

The first mention of the area in the "Official Records of the Navies" is a dispatch from Flag Officer McKean of the East Gulf Squadron to Sec. Welles, dated April 11, 1862, indicating that he sent the USS *Beauregard* north on a cruise:

> The schooner *Beauregard has been fitted as a gunboat, and sailed on the 29th ultimo* (29 March) *on a cruise. Being of light draft, I instructed her commander to examine the coast from Charlotte Harbor to St. Andrew's Bay. She is commanded by Acting Master David Stearns, with 1 acting master and 2 master's mates and*

a crew, in all of 19 men. Her armament consists of one 30-pounder Parrott rifle and two 12-pounder howitzers.

One of the routine duties of the squadron commander was to regularly issue reports to the Naval Secretary's office detailing "Stations of Vessels composing the East Gulf Blockading Squadron," indicating the status and location of all of the blockading vessels under his command. From September 1862 until January 1863 the reports of Flag Officers McKean and Lardner and Adm. Bailey indicate the steam gunboat USS *Penguin*, Lieutenant J.C. Williamson in command, maintained a blockade off Charlotte Harbor. She was replaced by the schooner USS *Wanderer* in January, to return to Key West for repair and refitting. The *Wanderer* maintained station there until sometime towards the end of February 1863, when she returned to Key West for refitting and was then sent north to patrol between Cedar Key and St. Marks. The schooner *J.S. Chambers* then took up station off Charlotte Harbor, with the schooner *Beauregard*, now under the command of Acting Ensign J.C. Hamlin, listed as "*Cruising between Cape Sable and Charlotte Harbor*" by mid-March. These two gunboats remained on station through early April.

The morning of April 6, 1863, the steam gunboat USS *Huntsville* was anchored offshore of Charlotte Harbor, steaming north after refitting at the Key West Naval Base. Like so many other Union gunboats, the *Huntsville* was a converted merchant steamer. On Christmas Eve 1861, she participated in the first ship-to-ship combat engagement at Mobile Bay, Alabama, trading fire with the Confeder-

Photo # NH 63876 Steamship Huntsville, which was USS Huntsville in 1861-1865. Artwork by Erik Heyl

Steam gunboat USS *Huntsville*. Artwork by Erik Heyl from Naval History and Heritage Command.

ate gunboat CSS *Florida* (also a converted steamer, not the later famed commerce raider). The ship was evidently steaming to a new station, under orders from the Navy Secretary, because the after action report from ship's captain, Acting Volunteer Lieutenant William C. Rogers, was addressed directly to Sec. Welles' attention, rather than a squadron commander. Rogers reported that his men sighted a sail bound south along the coast. The Union blockader captured the Confederate sloop *Minnie*, out of the Aucilla River, to the north. She was loaded with thirteen bales of cotton and evidently bound for Cuba.

Things appeared relatively quiet in the Charlotte Harbor region for the next couple of months, based on the lack of reports in the "Official Records of the Navies," until July 1863. On July 6, Acting Master W. R. Browne from the bark USS *Restless*, whom we got to know from his exploits destroying salt works in St. Andrews Bay later that year (Chapter 3) took on board two white refugees from the area. They told him that two Confederate blockade runners had attempted a run out that morning, but had evidently withdrawn. Browne sent out a party of 36 men in the bark's two cutters, under the command of Acting Ensigns Eason and Russel and Acting Master's Mate Browne, guided by the two refugees and well-armed. Their objective was to find the tender sloop USS *Rosalie*, with orders for her commander, Acting Ensign Charles P. Clark, and then with the *Rosalie* attempt to locate the runners.

The *Rosalie* was supposed to be stationed behind Pine Island, in Pine Island Sound. The boats from the *Restless* did not find the sloop in this location, and so they headed up the 'Peace Creek' (River) to the small settlement of Punta Gorda. With night falling, the boats anchored up for the evening. The next morning, they sighted the *Rosalie* about five miles upriver. Upon pulling up to the sloop, they were told by Ensign Clark that he had moved the sloop to the mouth of the river, hoping to link up with the refugees who had eventually made their way to the *Restless*. About 9 AM the morning of the sixth, he saw a sloop and a schooner making a run up the river (probably they had been on their way down, as reported by the refugees to Master Browne, when they sighted the Union gunboat and "turned tail"). He set off in pursuit, but it was his misfortune to ground the sloop on a sand bar in the river. The rebel runners continued upstream, no doubt having a better knowledge of the river channel. By the time the *Restless*' boats had reached the *Rosalie*, Clark had succeeded in freeing her from the bar. The boats and the sloop continued upriver, until shallow water would not allow the sloop to proceed further on the evening of the seventh.

Clark anchored for the night, at this time about 45 miles upriver. The next morning, July 8, Clark left the sloop in charge of Acting Master's Mate Browne of the *Restless* and took command of the two *Restless* boats and pushed further upriver to Horse Creek, where they found the two runners, unmanned. They were the Bahamian schooner *Ann* and an un-named sloop, both loaded with cotton. The naval expedition took possession of the two runners and their cargo and made their way back down to the *Rosalie*, then back out the bay to rejoin the *Restless* the afternoon of July 9. On the way downriver, Clark noted in his report to Master Browne that they were followed for some period by "guerillas" on the shoreline. For their actions, Adm. Bailey issued a letter of commendation to Acting Master Browne and the crew of the *Restless*, and promoted Ensign Clark from Acting Ensign to Acting Master.

Later in July 1863, the bark *Gem of the Sea* was reassigned from duty on the east coast of Florida to station off Charlotte Harbor on the Gulf coast. Capt. Baxter had been informed by refugees that there were a schooner and a sloop up the Caloosahatchee River. On July 27, 1863, he sent the sloop *Rosalie* and one of his launches up the river to cut them out. On July 29, they captured the British schooner *Georgie* in a small creek off the Caloosahatchee River near Fort Myers. They did not find a sloop. The schooner was unmanned and empty of cargo. She was in excellent condition, described by Baxter as "nearly new," and he requested permission to retain the ship as a second tender, along with the *Rosalie*. The bark then was involved in the capture of the sloop *Richard* in September.

Baxter was again given intelligence by refugees that a sloop loaded with cotton was lying up the Peace River. At noon on August 31, he sent a cutting out party consisting of the bark's launch and first cutter, with 22 men under the command of Acting Ensign W.H. Winslow and Acting Master's Mate Charles A. Edgcomb, and guided by one of the refugees. The party headed into the bay and that night found the sloop near the mouth of the Peace River. They boarded and found no one but a black Bahamian named Henry Brown. The sloop's cargo was 8½ bales of cotton. They returned to the *Gem of the Sea* the next morning and the sloop and cargo were made a prize and sent to Key West. During the expedition, one of the seamen was severely injured by the accidental discharge of a musket, and had to have his hand amputated. The *Gem of the Sea* continued on station off Charlotte Harbor for much of the rest of 1863-64 and captured additional prizes and prisoners.

In late 1863, Adm. Bailey was approached by Mr. Enoch Daniels, a refugee living in the Charlotte Harbor area, who requested permission to assemble a volunteer company from among the other Unionist refugees in the area and at Key West. They would form a Union raiding party that could work in conjunction with the U.S. Army and Navy, attacking, capturing and/or destroying rebel property and more importantly, attempting to disrupt the round-up and transport north of beef cattle to feed the southern armies. The U.S. Army would arm and equip this unit, and the Navy would transport them to embarkation points and lend them heavy gun support as long as they were within range, but at some point, this unit would move far enough inland to be beyond the Navy's support. This endeavor was approved, and Daniels formed a company of refugees designated by the Army as the "Florida Rangers," but Adm. Bailey liked to refer to them as the "Refugee Rangers."

Painting titled "*Cow Cavalry*" by Jackson Walker©. This shows a squad of rebel militia protecting their cattle from a Union raiding party (left background). Raids such as these were what the USN-organized Refugee Rangers were tasked with. Image used by permission.

In December 1863, the Rangers were ready to take the offensive. On December 24, Lt. Baxter of the *Gem of the Sea* sent an armed boat party of fourteen men in the ship's launch and cutter, under the command of Acting Ensign J.H. Jenks, to link up with Daniels and fifteen men of the Refugee Rangers at Useppa Island. The ship's landing party also towed with them two small boats for the Rangers' use. Daniels directed the landing party to a location on the Myakka

River ('Myacca' in the naval reports) to go ashore, where they landed on December 25. The Rangers headed inland to make trouble, while Jenks and his party of bluejackets established a defensive position on the beach to await the Rangers' return and evacuate them. The understanding was that the Rangers' party would be back in seven days. On December 28, the US Sloop *Rosalie* arrived at the landing site (sent there by Baxter) to help provide additional cover and fire support for Jenks' landing party. The next day they conducted additional reconnaissance in the area and relocated the USN shore camp to a location with a better defensive position.

Early the morning of December 30, the sailors heard noises in the brush adjacent to their camp, indicating "*. . . men were crawling toward them.*" Jenks at first thought it was Daniel's party returning to the landing site and he hailed, "*Who comes there?*" The reply came, "*Captain Daniels and his men.*" Jenks ordered them to halt and give the countersign agreed upon to confirm their identity. The response was a hail of musket and shotgun fire from what was estimated to be 40 rebels. The sailors returned fire and fell back to their boats. When they were out of the line of fire, the *Rosalie* opened up on the enemy troops with her 12-pdr boat howitzer with canister and grape and additional musket fire from seamen on the deck. The firepower of the *Rosalie* was invaluable and no doubt saved the lives of most of the USN landing party. Jenks returned to the *Gem of the Sea* with one wounded seaman and to reprovision. He was able to carry off all of the weapons, camp equipage and material from their beachhead with minimal loss.

Baxter sent the ship's boats and the *Rosalie* back to the landing site to await Daniel's return. On January 1, 1864, the sailors returned to the bark with Daniels and five of his men. Six of his original fifteen men had deserted after they landed on December 25, and it is likely that at least some of them were involved in the ambush of the USN shore party on December 30. Four were still "at large" ashore, having become separated from Daniel's party. These intrepid four eventually made their way over to the Peace River, found a small schooner, captured the ship and returned in it to the *Gem of the Sea*.

Even until the very end of the war, blockade runners always creatively looked for alternate locations to run their cargo into or out of the Florida coast. With Tampa Bay largely closed down by 1863-64, some looked to the south to the smaller, more remote Sarasota Bay. In late March 1864, the U.S. Schooner *Stonewall* was patrolling the passes into Sarasota Bay. Acting Master H.B. Carter had dispatched ship's boats into the bay to do some reconnaissance. Heavy weather created some difficulties in rendezvousing with his boats, but eventually they linked back up and the boats were sent out on March 24 to sound the channel through New Pass into the Bay. They found adequate water depths to accommodate the schooner, and Carter and his ship headed into the bay. The schooner grounded on shoal water once inside, then a lookout in the tops hailed the deck with a sighting of a sloop heading down the bay. Carter dispatched his boats to take the sloop, which turned out to be the *Josephine*, bound for Cuba from Tampa with seven bales of cotton.

Sketch by P.A. Sawyer of a Confederate blockade runner schooner. State Archives of Florida, Florida Memory Project.

Chapter 6. Actions in Tampa Bay and on the Big Bend Coast 1861-1864

Tampa Bay

Egmont Key, with its lighthouse, is located at the mouth of Tampa Bay. The blockade appears to have been established there by August 1861, when the steamer USS *R.R. Cuyler* and the schooner *Appleton* put in to the key for water. The light was deactivated by its keeper (sympathetic to the southern cause) about this time, when he removed the lens and other equipment to Tampa. At some point afterward, Union forces permanently occupied the key, and established it as a secondary base of operations for the East Gulf Blockading Squadron; providing a coaling station, water, and other basic repair

Egmont Key and its lighthouse. State Archives of Florida, Florida Memory Project.

and refitting facilities. It also provided a base of operations from which actions could be launched into Tampa Bay and the town of Tampa and was a refuge for Unionists evacuated there for protection.

The Confederate Army took over control of Ft. Brooke from Florida militia in mid-August 1861. Later that year, three 24-pdr guns were mounted in the fort, although some wanted to mount them at a small key that had more control of the mouth of the Hillsborough River. On April 13, 1862, the bark USS *Ethan Allen*, under the command of Acting Volunteer Lieutenant William B. Eaton, hove to off the fort. A bark was a three-masted sailing ship, with the fore and main masts fully square-rigged and the mizzen mast fore and aft-rigged. *Ethan Allan* was accompanied by the schooner USS *Beauregard*. Eaton was acting based on intelligence he had received from a Union sympathizer in the area named J. E. Whitehurst implying the fort could be easily taken. Eaton sent a message to the fort's commander, Confederate Major Robert B. Thomas, demanding the unconditional surrender of the fort and town, and indicating the navy ships would begin shelling the town after allowing a 24-hour period to evacuate women and children. Thomas replied that he appreciated the Lieutenant's consideration in allowing this evacuation, but he refused to surrender. After the grace period had passed, Eaton opened fire on the town with the *Ethan Allan's* 32-pdr guns and the *Beauregard's* 30-pdr rifled gun. The naval gunfire was intense, but evidently resulted in minimal damage and no civilian or Confederate military casualties. Receiving the report of this action, Flag Officer McKean, commanding the East Gulf Blockading Squadron, was evidently not pleased with Eaton, perhaps due to his threatening to fire on civilian targets. In his defense, Eaton replied:

> *You will, I have no doubt, overlook the error in judgement* (sic) *which I made, on taking into consideration the fact that I have been here with my vessel nearly six months, and after a long period of necessary inaction I was naturally anxious of giving my officers and men an opportunity of showing their mettle, and affording them the chance which they so much desired of doing something, if ever so little, toward crippling the enemy. . .*

Command of Ft. Brooke passed from Major Thomas to Captain John W. Pearson sometime in May-June 1862. Pearson was quite the colorful character; early in the war he had organized a company of troops known as the "Ocklawaha Rangers" and had conducted guerilla raids against Union forces along the St. Johns River, establishing a reputation as an audacious and bold fighter. On June 30, 1862, the USS *Sagamore* (*Unadilla*-Class gunboat) anchored off Ft. Brooke and trained her gunnery on the fort. Captain A. J. Drake sent a party of 20 sailors in the ship's launch under a flag of truce. Pearson met them on the water in one of his boats with 18 men. The officer commanding the *Sagamore's* boat, a Lieutenant, transmitted Capt. Drake's demand to surrender the fort and town. The flamboyant Confederate officer replied that he did not understand the meaning of the word. After being told of the consequences, he shot back a terse reply, foreshadowing U.S. Gen. Anthony McAuliffe's response of "*Nuts*" to a German request to surrender Bastogne in WW II. He told the USN officer to "*Pitch in.*" *Sagamore* opened fire on the fort and town at 6 PM that day. The fort's guns replied, scoring some hits on the ship, as it was anchored within their range, and may have forced Drake to call a halt to his ship's gunfire and move further offshore, out of range of the fort's guns. Drake resumed the bombardment the next day for a period of time. After a mid-day inter-

Unadilla-Class gunboat USS *Tahoma*. USS *Sagamore* would have looked similar. Artwork by R.G. Skerrett from Naval History and Heritage Command.

mission to the firing, Pearson had the Confederate battle flag hoisted over the fort, prompting the USN gunboat to fire a few more shells, but then eventually withdrawing. After this, Pearson realized the limitations of the existing guns at the fort and requested better cannons with longer range. When these were not forthcoming, he dispatched some members of his company to his workshop at Orange Springs and had them cast two rifled guns for use in the fort, although it appears these were never installed.

On October 26, 1862, the schooner USS *Beauregard* sailed into Tampa Bay under Confederate colors. To the surprise of Capt. Pearson and the citizens of Tampa (who thought it was a friendly ship), she hove to and commenced firing on the fort and town. The bombardment continued for much of the morning until the ship withdrew. In response to this, and the repeated harassment of the town by Union gunboats, Pearson looked for opportunities for revenge.

On March 27, 1863, the bark USS *Pursuit* sailed into the bay and prepared to shell the fort and town yet again. Pearson had a couple of his men don women's dresses and had them color their faces black to appear as refugee slaves. They built a small signal fire on the beach at Gadsden's Point and called to the *Pursuit* for help. The bark sent a ship's boat, under a white flag of truce, to retrieve the apparent escapees, but as the Union sailors drew near, the disguised rebels pulled out their weaponry and additional rebel troops emerged from hiding and demanded the surrender of the boat crew. Acting Master H.K. Lapham refused and asked the Confederates to respect the flag of truce. The rebels again demanded surrender, and when Lapham again refused, they commenced firing on the Union landing party. A number of seamen, along with Master Lapham, were wounded, but they managed to return the rebel fire and withdraw and return to the *Pursuit*, which fired four shells into the Confederate position. Acting Volunteer Lieutenant W. P. Randall, commanding the *Pursuit*, estimated that at least 100 Confederate troops were up against the men in his boat. Two days later the Union gunboats *Tahoma* and *Beauregard* sailed into the bay and shelled the fort and town in retaliation.

In the fall of 1863, Lt. Commander A. A. Semmes (cousin of the Confederate raider captain Raphael Semmes) of the USS *Tahoma* received intelligence that the rebel steamer *Scottish Chief* and sloop *Kate Dale* were up the Hillsborough River, loaded with cotton and ready to run the blockade. Joined by the side-wheel steam gunboat USS *Adela* (itself a captured and converted blockade runner), he dispatched six boats on October 16 with a force of 100 sailors and marines, plus officers and guides, under the command of his Executive Officer, Acting Master Thomas R. Harris. Landing near Ballast Point, the landing party at first tried to bring with them a small boat to cross the river, but eventually had to leave the boat in a hiding place, due to the difficulty of transporting it. Master Harris wrote in his after action report:

Captured Confederate blockade runner USS *Adela*. Drawing by crewmember George H. Rodgers. Naval History and Heritage Command.

After this we moved along very rapidly under the direction of our excellent guides, and reached the banks of the Hillsboro (sic) River about 4 a.m. October 17, having marched about 14 miles. Having stationed lookouts, the party lay down till daylight. Shortly after daylight we discovered the steamer and sloop on the opposite side of the river about 9 miles above us. The force was immediately moved to a point opposite of where they lay and those on board ordered to send a boat to us. When the boat reached [us] I sent Acting Ensigns Randall and Balch, with a suitable number of men, on board of the vessels, where they made prisoners of all except two, who escaped on the Tampa side. Hauling the vessels over, I fired both effectually.

The landing party returned to the beach area where they came ashore, and boats were dispatched from the gunboats to retrieve them. The Confederates had by now been alerted to the presence of the naval landing party, and sent troops to pursue them. An intense firefight ensued between the navy men and rebel troops, a mix of infantry and dismounted cavalry. Union casualties were three killed, six wounded, and four taken prisoner.

U.S.S. STONEWALL.   U.S.S. JAMES L. DAVIS.   U.S.S. SUNFLOWER.

USN blockading gunboats off Tampa Bay. State Archives of Florida, Florida Memory Project.

Some smaller, but important, salt works were located in Tampa Bay. On June 7, 1864, the steam gunboat USS *Sunflower* sent three boats ashore to destroy a works consisting of four large kettles and furnaces, along with a quantity of salt. On July 11, 1864, a landing party from the bark USS *James L. Davis* destroyed a works consisting of eight boilers, producing 150 bushels of salt per day. A second expedition from the *Davis* was conducted on July 16 to another works with four boilers, which were destroyed.

In May 1864 the USS *Sunflower* rendezvoused with the steam gunboat *Honduras* and the USS *J.L. Davis*. The *Honduras* carried troops that were landed with a naval force of 54 men on May 5, taking possession of Tampa and Ft. Brooke. The naval landing party raised the Union flag over Tampa, which remained in Union hands until the war's end. In July 1864, the Headquarters of the East Gulf Blockading Squadron was temporarily moved to Tampa, due to a severe outbreak of yellow fever in Key West. Adm. Bailey stepped down from his position as squadron commander in August 1864 due to ill health. Capt. Theodore P. Greene assumed temporary command of the squadron at that time, and in October 1864, Acting Rear Adm. C. K. Stribling took command of the East Gulf Squadron.

The Lower Big Bend

The Anclote River drains into the Gulf of Mexico just north of Tampa Bay, at the southern end of what is know as the "Big Bend" coast of Florida (stretching from the Anclote to the St. Marks River).

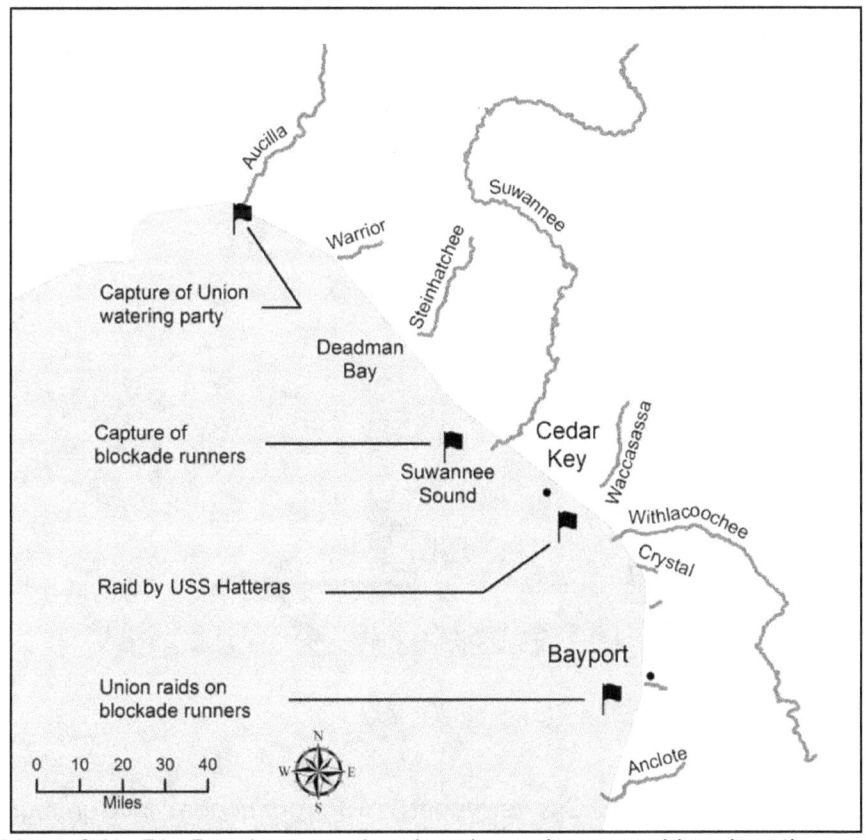

Map of the Big Bend coast, showing rivers, bays, and key locations of naval events.

The schooner USS *Two Sisters* patrolled off the river in 1863-64. On July 7, 1864, the schooners *Ariel*, *Sea Bird*, *Stonewall*, and sloop *Rosalie* took on 260 army troops and landed them on the north side of the river. This force then proceeded north towards Brooksville, engaging a small force of Confederate home guard in what became known as the "Brooksville Raid," which is observed at a re-enactment the third weekend of January each year at the Sand Hill Boy Scout Camp near Brooksville.

On March 28, 1863, the USS *Sagamore*, under the command of Lt. Commander Earl English, rendezvoused at Cedar Key with the gunboat USS *Fort Henry*, commanded by Acting Lieutenant Edward Yorke McCauley. The *Fort Henry* was a side-wheel steamer that was a New York City ferryboat before the war. Purchased by the Navy in March 1862 and modified into a gunboat, the *Fort Henry* was one of a number of New York ferryboats to serve in the Union Navy during the war. Although they were not particularly seaworthy, these tough little ships were well suited to inshore blockade work along the rivers and bays of the southern coastline due to their shallow draft and their double-ended design (they could steam in either direction, forward or back, without having to turn around). Because they were already built to carry heavy loads, they did not require a great deal of modification

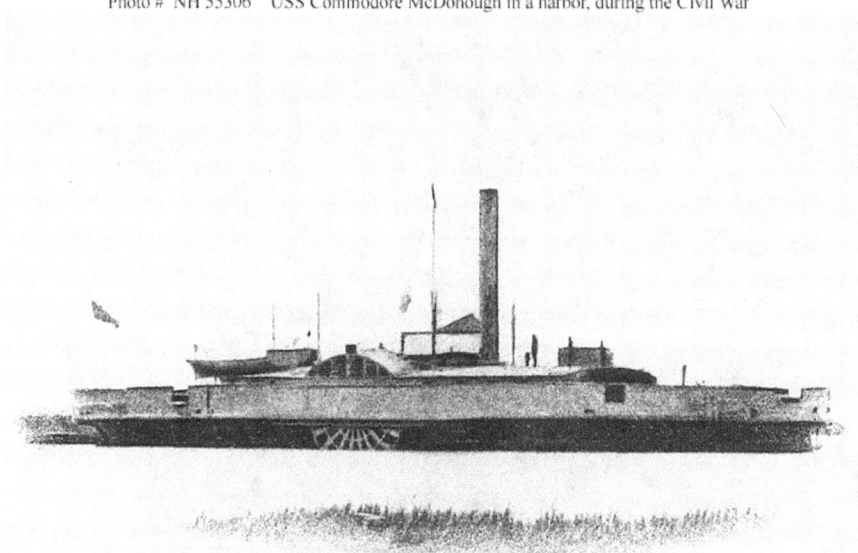

Photo # NH 55306 USS Commodore McDonough in a harbor, during the Civil War

Converted New York City ferryboat USS *Commodore McDonough*. USS *Fort Henry* would have looked similar. Naval History and Heritage Command.

to mount heavy gunnery on their fore and aft decks. Under McCauley's command, the *Fort Henry* earned a reputation as the "terror of the coast," as described by Adm. Bailey, capturing one sloop in 1862 and four schooners, four sloops, and a scow in 1863, along with destroying or forcing the destruction of a number of other blockade runners and conducting shore party raids.

On April 2, 1863, a boat expedition set out from the USS *Sagamore*, under the command of Lt. McCauley. This consisted of sailors and marines in two launches from the USS *St. Lawrence* (which had joined the *Sagamore* earlier), a launch and cutter from the *Sagamore*, a launch and cutter from the *Fort Henry*, and an additional cutter with the *Fort Henry's* surgeon to act as an ambulance boat. Their objective was a cutting-out expedition to go after an unknown number of blockade runners anchored in the harbor of Bayport, north of Tampa Bay, at the mouth of the Weeki Wachee River. The boat party found several blockade runners in the harbor. Heavy weather had slowed the progress of the USN raiders, which enabled their approach to be spotted by Confederate forces on shore. The rebels had run the smaller ships (two small schooners and two sloops) far inshore and aground. A larger schooner, loaded with cotton, was still moored out in the main part of the harbor. McCauley sent one of the *Sagamore's* boats after another sloop at anchor, the Sloop *Helen*, which they captured and burned. This ship was loaded with corn. As they approached the larger schooner, a small Confederate battery of two field guns, along with riflemen entrenched in the surrounding forests, opened fire on the boat expedition. Someone was seen leaving the schooner, and shortly flames and smoke began to be visible from this ship.

The larger launches were each armed with a Dahlgren boat howitzer mounted on the bow. The Dahlgren howitzer, named after its designer, Capt. John A. Dahlgren of the Bureau of Naval Ordnance, was a superb field piece specifically designed to be used by naval personnel for shore party raids, ship defense, etc. The barrel could be easily dismounted from its carriage and mounted on a fitting on the bow of a ship's boat to provide fire support as the boat approached land. On shore, it could be remounted on the carriage and towed by hand to provide fire support. The howitzer was made in 12-pdr and 24-pdr versions. The launches from the *Sagamore* and *Fort Henry* engaged the battery with their 24-pdr howitzers, and their fire was effective enough to drive the battery's gun crews away. The launches then directed their gunfire towards the rifle positions. The firing of the howitzers was so rapid that two of them were dismounted

Replica of a 12-pdr Dahlgren boat howitzer at the Ft. Caroline National Monument. Note fitting on the bottom of the barrel enabling quick removal and mounting on bow of ship's boat. Author's photo.

and could no longer be used. One seaman from the *Sagamore* was hit by a musket ball during the engagement, but was not injured severely. The large schooner loaded with cotton continued burning and was completely destroyed.

Seeing that they had largely accomplished their mission to capture, destroy or disable the blockade runners, McCauley had the boat expedition pull offshore out of range of the rebel gunners for rest and food. The raiding party then proceeded north up the coast to the Chassahowitzka River, where they took shelter for the night inside the river mouth. A strong gale continued to blow and all of the boats took on much water, which kept men baling in shifts all night. Some of the powder charges for the howitzers were soaked with seawater and rendered useless. The next morning, the party continued north to the Crystal River, which they searched for blockade runners. Again, it appears their coming was known, because they found no ships to capture or destroy in the areas they searched, their having been moved to safer anchorages. They then headed south and investiga-

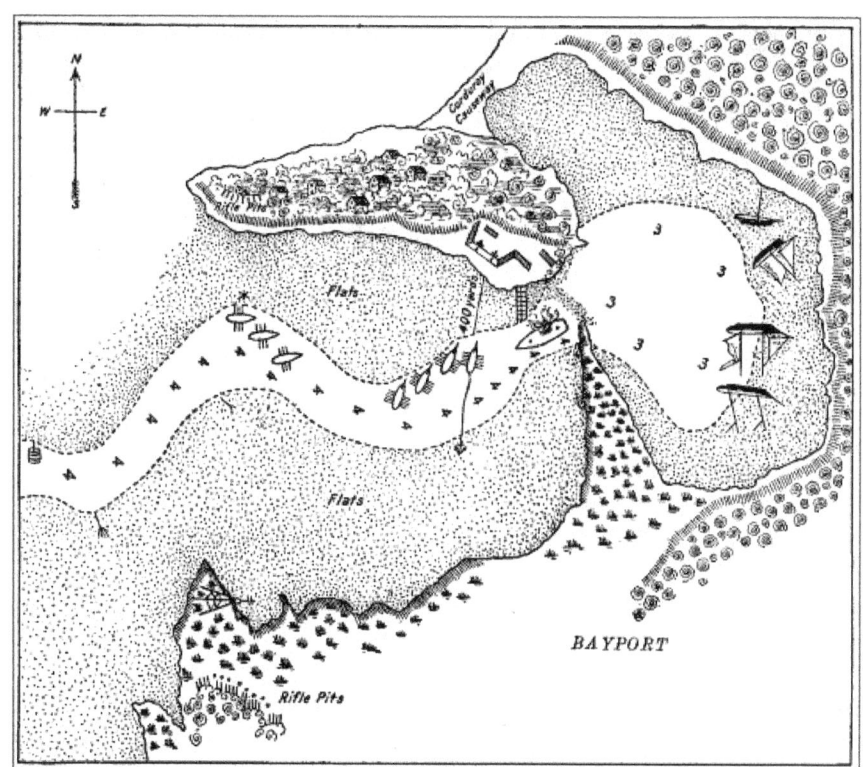

Map showing configuration of Bayport harbor, showing locations of Confederate defenses and blockade runners. From the Official Records of the Union and Confederate Navies in the War of the Rebellion.

ted the Homosassa River, then back north and checked up the Withlacoochee River. They took shelter there during the night in an abandoned house to dry out and rest. They continued north the next day to check out the Waccasassa River, and finally arrived back at the *Fort Henry* off Cedar Key the evening of April 7. The boat expedition had lasted five days and covered an estimated 75 miles.

In early June 1863, ship's boats from the *Fort Henry* captured the sloop *Emma* off Seahorse Key. Having need of an extra boat, now Lt. Commander McCauley kept the sloop instead of sending it to Key West for adjudication as a prize. Marine Orderly Sgt. Christopher Nugent had the sloop repaired and fitted out to transport his marines, and on June 15, 1863, Sgt. Nugent and six marines from the *Fort Henry's* guard undertook an expedition up the Crystal River. About six miles upriver, Nugent spotted a log breastworks. Landing with a party of four marines, Nugent and his men drove away the detachment of eleven rebels manning the small fortification. Nugent was hit, but not injured, by a pistol shot from the officer commanding the militia as they retreated. He ordered his marines to hold their fire due to the presence of a woman in the midst of the enemy troops as they retreated. The marines carried off the small arms found in the works and destroyed the other material found there which they could not remove. After receiving McCauley's report of these actions, Adm. Bailey of the East Gulf Squadron wrote to Sec. Welles:

> I would respectfully suggest whether the conduct of Orderly Sergeant Nugent does not bring him within that class of men who should receive the medal of honor authorized by Congress to be given to 'such petty officers, seamen, and marines as shall most distinguish themselves by gallantry in action,' etc.

On April 16, 1864, Marine Sgt. Nugent was awarded the Medal of Honor for his actions at Crystal River.

A second expedition to Bayport was conducted in August-September 1863, under Lt. Commander Semmes of the USS *Tahoma*. In this case Adm. Bailey had requested the use of the captured shallow draft steamer *James Battle* from the Army. Semmes and the *Battle* set out from Key West on August 23. Initially he and his crew tried to cut out a rebel steamer up the Suwannee River, but shallow depths precluded this (they were aground for a period of twelve days). At Cedar Key, the *Battle* took in tow a launch from the USS *Fort Henry* and two sloops, the *Annie* and *Two Sisters* (the former with Lt. Commander McCauley aboard, who had led an earlier expedition into the harbor). They then headed south and descended upon the harbor of Bayport. Anchoring off the inner harbor at Bayport, Semmes and McCauley went in with two cutters and a launch armed with a Dahlgren howitzer. Eventually Semmes spotted a steamer in his telescope, camouflaged with tree branches to blend in with the shoreline forests. By the time the landing party approached the steamer, it was observed to be set ablaze by the rebels. A warehouse loaded with cotton was also apparently set ablaze, as Semmes reported he could smell the characteristic odor of burning cotton. The expedition returned to Cedar Key, and Semmes and the *Battle* departed for Key West on September 17, bringing along some captured slaves, lumber and iron.

Cedar Keys/Suwannee River

The Cedar Keys, on the Gulf Coast of Florida (consisting of Way, Depot/Atsena Otie, Seahorse, Snake, and North Keys), was an important port at the start of the Civil War, in part because a newly constructed rail line connected the port to interior parts of the state and ran all the way up to Fernandina on the Atlantic coast. Seahorse Key had a light station (constructed in 1856 under the direction of then Lt. George Gordon Meade) which guided ships into the Port of Cedar Key and the nearby mouth of the Suwannee River. The Town of Cedar Key itself was located on Atsena Otie Key.

On January 16, 1862, the Union gunboat USS *Hatteras* hove to off Cedar Key and debarked ships boats, which entered the harbor and burned four schooners, three sloops, a scow, a sailboat, and a launch. Some of the schooners were loaded with cotton, turpentine, rosin, and lumber, ready to run the blockade. The railroad depot and wharf, seven railroad cars, the telegraph station and a storehouse were also burned, and arms and equipment confiscated. To add to all this, the ship's crew captured most of a small Confederate garrison manning a gun battery on Seahorse Key, including the officer and thirteen soldiers. Needless to say, the bluejackets of the *Hatteras* earned their pay that day.

Seahorse key and its lighthouse. State Archives of Florida, Florida Memory Project.

Not long after *Hatteras* departed, the USS *Tahoma* arrived off Seahorse Key on February 1, 1862, and commenced shelling the battery, just in case it had been reoccupied. Ship's boats were sent ashore and the battery was found abandoned, with the destruction wrought by the crew of *Hatteras* still evident. For the remainder of the war, Seahorse Key with its lighthouse (which had been disabled by the Confederates) remained under Union control, and was used as an additional secondary base of operations by the East Gulf Blockading Squadron (along with Egmont Key), depriving the Confederacy of the use of Cedar Key as a port for the remainder of the War.

A major task of the men and ships of the East Gulf Blockading Squadron was the location and destruction of Confederate salt works along the Florida Gulf coast (Chapter 3). During the latter part of 1862, USS *Tahoma* and USS *Somerset* (like *Fort Henry*, a converted New York City ferryboat) patrolled the waters around the Cedar Keys. After receiving intelligence from escaped slaves that Confederate troops in the area had been withdrawn, and knowing of the existence and location of a sizable salt works on Depot Key, Lt. Commander Earl English brought his ship the *Somerset* close inshore on October 4, 1862, and began shelling the facility with the ship's guns. On seeing a white flag hoisted, he dispatched two ship's boats under the command of Acting Master Dennison, his Executive Officer. When they landed, they began to break up some of the salt boilers and approached a house over which the white flag flew with "several women," which made the bluejackets hold their fire. Lt. Cdr. English reported:

> *No sooner, however, had his* (Dennison's) *men gotten out of the boats to destroy the works than they were fired upon by some 25 persons concealed in the rear. He returned the fire, killing and wounding several.*

English continued with his report, noting that prior to withdrawing, the landing party ". . . *destroyed several barrels of salt, a number of boats; captured one launch and a large flat.*" There were no sailors killed in this action, but several were wounded. The report of the ship's surgeon, Dr. L.J. Draper, indicated two sailors "wounded dangerously," four "wounded seriously," and two "wounded slightly."

The *Tahoma* arrived on the scene later that day (Commander J.C. Howell, captain), and on October 6, a large landing party (eight boats and about 111 men), armed with two Dahlgren boat howitzers,

Salt boiler replica, Panama City. Author's photo.

went ashore to the works. After deploying the howitzers and firing shell, shrapnel and canister into the works, driving off the Confederate defenders, the landing party spread out in skirmish order and began their destructive work. Cdr. Howell reported that a total of 50 to 60 salt boilers were destroyed (estimated by Lt. Cdr. English to produce 150 bushels of salt a day working around the clock), and all structures at the site were burned to the ground in retaliation for the ambush attack on the Union landing party on October 4. As the USN forces withdrew to their ships, a train carrying Confederate reinforcements arrived at Cedar Key and the gray troops deployed and fired on the landing party with muskets, but by then the USN boats were out of range. No seamen or marines were killed or injured in this larger expedition. Cdr. Howell sharply punctuated his after-action report to the East Gulf Squadron command by noting that, "*The rebels here needed a lesson and they have had it.*" Officers of both ships were highly complementary of the conduct of their men during these raids.

On July 20, 1863, a launch was dispatched at dawn from the USS *Fort Henry*, lying off the Cedar Keys. The boat was under the command of Chief Boatswain's Mate Gillespie. Ordinarily, an officer would be in command of the boat, but two of Lt. Commander

McCauley's officers were down with illness, a third was taking a prize to Key West and a fourth was needed on the gunboat. The mission of this boat expedition was to pull south towards Bayport and once again locate and intercept any blockade runners. Gillespie was specifically ordered not to proceed up Crystal River due to the suspected presence of rebel militia. As they cruised south past the mouth of the Waccasassa River, just south of Cedar Keys, the bluejackets spotted bales of cotton floating out of the river into the bay. With visions of prize money clouding their judgment, they proceeded up the Waccasassa, hoping to capture more. As they pulled through an area where the river channel narrowed, the boat was fired upon by an ambush of as many as 50 or 60 rebel troops. Seaman Patrick Doran was hit in the neck and died instantly. Seaman John Bishop was also hit and died shortly afterward. The remaining seamen returned fire and pulled the boat back downriver out of range. As might be expected, McCauley was not at all pleased when the boat returned, indicating in his report to Adm. Bailey, "*I forbade the ascent of Crystal River, little imagining a necessity of the kind in respect to the*

Sketch of the USS *Fort Henry* off Seahorse Key. By the author.

Waccasassa." Seamen Doran and Bishop were buried in a small cemetery on Seahorse Key. Their graves can be viewed today when the key is open to the public on certain days of high tides.

In early December 1863, the US Schooner *Fox* was patrolling off the mouth of the Suwannee River, just north of Cedar Keys. Acting Master George Ashbury, commanding, anchored the ship off the mouth of the river on December 19, probably to give his crew some rest and time to do repair work after weathering a fierce storm on December 10. The late morning of December 20, the lookout hailed the deck to report a steamer anchored a few miles up the coast. Ashbury made sail, got underway and approached to within three miles of the steamer. He sent a boat ahead to sound a channel for the schooner to follow; for awhile this enabled him to get closer to the steamer, but eventually the schooner grounded in about 8½ feet of water. While they were making their way toward it, they could see boats shuttling between the steamer and the shore. After getting off the shoal and anchoring, Ashbury opened fire on the steamer with one or both of the schooner's 12-pdr guns (most likely the "rifle", since it would have been more accurate at long-range than the other, which was a smoothbore gun). He sent an armed ship's boat under the command of Acting Ensign Jackson to the steamer. Jackson and his men boarded the ship and found her abandoned, empty of cargo, and with no identifying papers. The machinery was still warm, suggesting a recent arrival. She was a side-wheel steamboat, painted "a light lead color" with black smokestack, obviously as a form of camouflage to evade detection at night. Jackson set torches to the ship, and by the time he returned to the *Fox* it appeared to be burning thoroughly. The ship was anchored in the channel leading into the mouth of the Suwannee, which Jackson described as "*being very narrow in places and extremely intricate.*" The channel was well-marked with stakes, which Jackson and his men pulled up as they returned to the *Fox*. The steamer was eventually determined to be the *Powerful*, of English registry. A USN boarding party subsequently went to the burned steamer to destroy as much of its machinery as possible to prevent salvage by the rebels.

A few days later, the afternoon of December 24, the *Fox* sighted a sail off the Suwannee. After a chase of a couple hours, during which the *Fox* fired several warning shots, the other schooner hove to by hauling down its jib sail. Ashbury ordered the other ship to lower its big foresail and send over one of its boats (the seas evidently being too heavy for his small ship's boat), but the other ship turned and made a run at the *Fox*, "playing chicken" as it were. The other schooner struck the *Fox*, carrying away some of the boat davits.

Ashbury ordered one of his guns to fire on the other schooner, the shot striking its captain in the leg while he was at the schooner's helm. Acting Ensign Jackson was sent on board. The ship had no papers (they had been thrown overboard by the schooner's captain), but was eventually determined to be the British schooner *Edward*. Ashbury sent the schooner to Key West as a prize, under the command of Ensign Jackson.

On February 26, 1864, Acting Volunteer Lieutenant R.B. Smith of the USS *Nita* (a side-wheel steamboat which was yet another captured and converted blockade runner), reported sighting a steamer running down the East Pass of the mouth of the Suwannee River. The *Nita* was on station off the West Pass, but lookouts in the tops of the gunboat were able to spy the runner coming down in the East Pass. Smith got his ship's steam up and went after the runner, weaving between the abundant oyster reefs present at the mouth of the Suwannee. He had ship's boats run out and they also participated in the chase. At some point during the chase, they saw the runner go aground and begin throwing bales of cotton overboard. They also observed her officers and crew abandoning the vessel, and by the time they drew near, it was fully engulfed in flames, having been set on fire by its abandoning crew. This was evidently the third time this steamer had attempted a run through the blockade, as Smith reported seeing the steamer twice make a run down West Pass, then return upstream to safety after seeing the Union blockade ship at the mouth of West Pass. She finally decided to make a run down East Pass, but it was unsuccessful. The runner burned to the waterline and was destroyed.

The Upper Big Bend

In mid-1862, the US Bark *Kingfisher* patrolled the Florida Gulf coast off the upper Big Bend. *Kingfisher* had been acquired by the U.S. Navy in August 1861 and reconfigured as a sailing gunboat, armed with four VIII (8)-inch Dahlgren smoothbore guns and assigned to the East Gulf Blockading Squadron. The ship was under the command of Acting Master Joseph P. Couthouy. In those days, an ample supply of potable fresh water was an extremely vital need for a blockade ship patrolling Florida's subtropical gulf coast. The heat sapped sailors' strength as they worked the ship and trained, necessitating the availability of abundant water for hydrating, and water was even more vitally needed on shore party raids. In the case of a steam ship, this was not an issue, as plenty of fresh water could be distilled from seawater using the ship's boilers. But for a sailing ship on blockade, fresh water had to be brought to the ship, or the rivers draining to the coast were the main source for replenishing a ship's water supply, although the threat of ambush by local partisan guerillas was always present. With the ship's water supply getting dangerously low (and what remained getting very foul and contaminated), Couthouy anchored off the Aucilla River in early May 1862 and decided to try to get fresh water there.

Because of the threat of ambush, the first week of May 1862, Couthouy sent Masters Mate C.E. Sloan to conduct a reconnaissance up the river, accompanied by a local pilot, to scout out potential locations for a landing party to refill the ship's water casks. Sloan found an abandoned woodcutters camp about two miles above the mouth of the river. Couthouy reported:

> *He* (Sloan) *reported it as perfectly secure, showing no token of having been inhabited for years. It was long ago a resort of live-oak cutters, and quantities of the timber were yet scattered along the banks. The whole region was covered with undergrowth and jungle, and the pilot, Welles, assured me the place had been deserted since the last Indian War, and was inaccessible by any land route.*

Continuing to act with caution, Couthouy dispatched small woodcutting parties to the location between May 5-10 to see if guerillas were present in the area. Finally, on May 27, a landing party of two ship's boats with water casks were sent in to the location. They returned with 480 gallons of fresh water and three additional trips were made in the immediate days afterward. On June 2, another watering party of three boats was dispatched up the river, led by the pilot Welles, and under the command of Acting Master S.C. Curtis. The two ship's boats headed upriver to the watering site, while the pilot remained at the river mouth in his own small sailboat to do some fishing. When the pilot arrived upriver at the landing site, Couthouy reported that:

> *. . . as he* (Welles) *approached the landing, he saw a number of our casks in the river and close to the landing, the second cutter capsized, and surmised at once that our people had been surprised by the enemy. The first cutter was nowhere to be seen. After reconnoitering cautiously, seeing no one, he ventured to right the se-*

cond cutter and make her fast to a tree, and to roll the casks up on the bank, when he observed several breastworks of heavy logs that had been erected since Saturday, and fearing the enemy might yet be in the vicinity, prudently made the best of his way back to the ship.

After receiving the pilot's report, Couthouy sent Masters Mate Sloan out the night of June 3 to scout the area under cover of darkness, retrieve the remaining ship's boat, and most importantly, determine if any of the landing party had escaped and were in hiding during the day, hoping for a night rescue. Sloan returned the morning of June 4 and reported that he found two dead seamen (Antoine Faulkner, Seaman, and Antonio Euphrates, Ordinary Seaman), but not the remainder of the landing party. Couthouy then knew that the rest of his men had been taken prisoner.

He dispatched Masters Mate Sloan under a flag of truce to the Confederate garrison at the nearby St. Marks lighthouse on June 5, to inquire as to the status of his men and the possibilities of sending them clothing and supplies, and with a letter with instructions for Master Curtis. He also asked for the terms of the truce to include the ability to properly bury the two dead seamen and mark their graves, as Sloan had only interred them in shallow, temporary graves when he found them a couple days earlier. A series of diplomatic exchanges occurred between Couthouy, Lt. D.W. Gwynn, commanding Confederate forces at Camp Jackson, near St. Marks, Lt. C.P. McGary of the C.S. Navy, and Confederate Gen. Finegan regarding the affairs of the captured USN seamen. Couthouy and Gwynn actually met personally in small boats at a buoy off the St. Marks River to discuss matters. Gwynn specifically mentioned the tenacious fight the bluejackets had put up, expressing his admiration for their bravery. Couthouy subsequently requested the squadron commander convene a formal hearing on this affair to insure that he had acted properly. Newly appointed Flag Officer J. L. Lardner decided simply to admonish him to, "... *be more careful in the future.*"

On February 17, 1864, Lt. Commander David Harmony, commanding the USS *Tahoma*, was on blockade station off the St. Marks River. Somehow he learned of the existence of a sizable salt works to the east, on the Big Bend coast near the "Warrior River" (present-day Spring Warrior Creek, north of the Steinhatchee River/Deadman's Bay), about 40 miles east of his station. He dispatched a boat expedition under the command of his Executive Officer Acting Master E.C. Weeks. Interestingly, this expedition consisted of 20 of

Harmony's men, plus at least 96 "refugees" – local Unionist sympathizers, whom Weeks had met with the day before to see if they were interested in participating in this expedition. The boat expedition met Weeks and the refugees at the mouth of the Warrior River. Weeks took some of the men and the refugees and marched inshore to the works, where they began to destroy them. The remainder of the landing party, under the command of Acting Ensign J.G. Koehler, sailed further to the east (and possibly south) and landed. Both USN landing parties started to destroy an extensive series of salt works that extended along the length of the shoreline here. Harmony reported:

> He (Koehler) *commenced destroying on the eastern end of the long line of works, which extended about 7 miles, working up to where the other party were employed. After effectually destroying everything they could lay hands upon, the party started to return at about 10 a.m., Saturday, marching all night, arriving here this morning at about 9 o'clock, having marched over 80 miles by forced marches, and rowed some 30 miles.*

On March 2, 1864, Acting Master James S. Williams, commanding the U.S. Schooner *Annie*, was on blockade station in Deadman's Bay, off the Steinhatchee River. This is north up the Big Bend Coast from the Suwannee River/Cedar Keys area, about halfway between the Suwannee and St. Marks Rivers. Williams submitted a report to his immediate superior, Lt. Commander Harmony of the USS *Tahoma*:

> *Sir: I herewith respectfully submit the following report of the destruction of a fine schooner at this place:*
> *I came to anchor at 9 a.m., with a strong norther blowing, distant about 5 miles from land, and at 11 a.m. made a small boat standing out for us. Set English colors at masthead* (this was a ruse used by the USN blockader to trick the small boat). *At 12 the boat put back and I gave chase with the schooner, setting the American ensign. At 12:30 p.m. made a schooner inside the reefs and stood for her until 1:10 p.m., when we anchored in 6 feet of water (having gained rapidly on the small boat), manned our boat with 5 men in charge of Master's Mate James T. Bowling to board the schooner. At 1:45 the chased boat was seen to go on board and after stopping about ten minutes were seen to fire the schooner and*

leave. At 2 our boat boarded the schooner and found her to be a new schooner of about 80 tons (lying ashore) and loaded with an assorted cargo, amongst which was a large quantity of ammunition. Our boat remained on board but a short time, as the fire was making great headway, and in about three minutes after their leaving a heavy explosion took place blowing out her decks. At 3:30 boat returned on board, and at 4 a small skiff was seen coming off with a white flag flying. At 4:15 the skiff came alongside and contained 1 man, calling himself Allen A. Stephens, and wished ammunition, saying he belonged to a company of 20 men about to rise against the rebel Government. I allowed the man Stephens to go on shore again and told him I would report the case up the coast. Stephens says the schooner burned arrived here on the 29th ultimo (that is, 29 February).

On May 28, 1864 the U.S. Schooner *Fox* was patrolling the waters between the Suwannee and St. Marks Rivers. Off the Taylor County coastline north of Deadman's Bay, they sighted plumes of smoke, indicating the location of a salt works. Acting Master Charles Chase sent a party of bluejackets ashore:

On the 28th May I sent a boat from this vessel with an armed crew, Acting Ensign Jackson in charge, to reconnoiter the shore, and if practicable, to destroy the works. The persons employed at the place fled at the sight of the boat. Mr. Jackson landed with 8 men and destroyed 25 salt kettles of a capacity of 150 gallons each, with all the pumps, tools, and 100 bushels of clean salt. On the 5th instant I landed a party about 10 miles above Deadman's Bay and destroyed another of these works, with 27 kettles of about 200 gallons capacity each (these were new kettles, and finely porcelained (sic) *or cemented inside), and burned all the houses, five in number, with a large quantity of tools, carts, etc.*

Subsequently, Chase sent Ensign Jackson up the Suwannee River, where he found a stash of ten bales of cotton near Clay Landing. These were confiscated and stored on a small island near the mouth of the river for later retrieval. On June 23, 1864, Adm. Bailey sent orders to Acting Master Thomas Chatfield commanding the sloop USS *Dale* to retrieve the cotton:

SIR: On receipt of this you will proceed with the **Two Sisters** *to secure a quantity of cotton captured up the Suwanee* (sic) *River by the tender* **Fox**. *Mr. Chase states that it consists of 7 good bales and three or four broken ones, and may be found on a key at the north side of the West Pass of the Suwanee River, to the northward of and in sight of the wreck of the steamer* **Powerful**. *You will place this cotton in charge of the senior officer at Cedar Keys to be forwarded to Key West by the first opportunity, and you will yourself attend to having it legibly marked, that it may not be mistaken for any other lot.*

Chapter 7. The War Ends – Actions in 1865 and Concluding Thoughts

Northeast Florida

After their defeat at the Battle of Olustee in February 1864, the Union Army retreated back to Jacksonville and established defensive works there. They remained there until the end of the war in 1865, continuing to be protected by the guns of the U.S. Navy on the St. Johns River, as well as their own artillery in extensive earthworks. They conducted small raids into the interior of the state to continue harassing actions and to confiscate property and free slaves.

City of Jacksonville waterfront, post-war. State Archives of Florida, Florida Memory Project.

Fernandina and St. Augustine were continuously occupied by Union forces from 1862 to the end of the war, and were never evacuated for periods of time, as Jacksonville was. St. Augustine was used mostly as a rest area for Union troops, and was never particularly heavily garrisoned by the U.S. Army. Buker credits this to the "inside blockade" maintained there by the U.S. Navy, including the presence of USN gunboats on the St. Johns River and adjacent coastal waters, which provided fire support and destroyed numerous small boats, launches, scows, etc. which frustrated the efficient movement of rebel troops on the adjacent river.

Union Navy gunboat patrols on the St. Johns River continued through the end of the war, providing security to U.S. Army movements along the river. Based on the lack of reports in the Official Records of the Navies, much of 1865 appears to have been quiet on the St. Johns River except for the capture of some USN personnel in April. On April 6, 1865, a boat was dispatched from the USS *Ottawa* with Second Assistant Engineer George H. White, Acting Assistant Surgeon Lewis H. Willard, Coal Heaver Lewis S. Smith, and Ship's Nurse Andrew Farley. The purpose of their expedition was for Dr. Willard to attend to the illness of a Mrs. Douglass, staying at the home of Mr. Reed in Mandarin. When the party did not return that evening, the gunboat's captain Lt. Commander James Stillwell sent Acting Ensign Walter N. Smith with an armed boat party to Mr. Reed's and found out they had been captured by scouts from the Second Florida Cavalry, C.S. Army. Eventually, they were paroled in a prisoner exchange.

After the war, steamboat Capt. Jacob Brock was paroled and was able to reacquire the steamer *Darlington* and resume his occupation running steamboats on the St. Johns River. He built a hotel at Enterprise, Florida, on Lake Monroe near current-day Sanford, to where he ferried guests aboard his steamboats. Other owners and captains were able to rebuild their pre-war steamboat fleets and resume their occupations carrying passengers, mail, and freight on the river. Ulysses S. Grant and Robert E. Lee both took sightseeing trips on St. Johns River steamboats after the war.

The Panhandle

After its abandonment by the Confederate Army in May 1862, the Pensacola Navy Yard and Forts Barrancas, McCree and Pickens

Steamboat captain Jacob Brock, probably after the war. State Archives of Florida, Florida Memory Project.

remained in Union hands until the end of the war. The West Gulf Blockading Squadron operated out of the Navy Yard and continued the blockade of the west Florida coast and the Gulf coast to the Texas/Mexico border. The Navy Yard was a critically important coaling, resupply and repair base for the squadron. In early January 1865, Union Army forces were burgeoning in Pensacola as they prepared for a massive invasion of Alabama and assault on the City of Mobile. Large docks in the navy yard that had been destroyed when the rebels evacuated were repaired to enable the landing of cavalry, locomotives, rolling stock, rails, and other heavy equipment to support the invasion of Alabama. The invasion began in mid-March 1865 and by mid-April, Mobile had fallen, the last major Confederate city to be taken.

On January 16, 1865, a boat expedition set out from the US Bark *Midnight*. The expedition was under the command of Acting Master Charles H. Cadieu. They travelled in the *Midnight's* launch and second cutter with a Dahlgren boat howitzer. Their main objective was to capture or destroy a steamer that ran between Columbus, Georgia

Pensacola Navy Yard, 1865. State Archives of Florida, Florida Memory Project.

and "Rickoe's Bluff" on the Apalachicola River, transporting supplies to aid the Confederate Army. Master Cadieu and his men set out from St. Andrews Bay, went up the Wetappo River to a landing, and made their way overland to an area of safety they knew as the "salt house." They were lead by a local guide, and met three more Unionists at the salt house by a prior arrangement. These linked them up with another local Unionist who lent them a wagon with two oxen to transport their cutter overland. They made their way over to the Chipola River, arriving late in the evening of January 18. The morning of the 19th, they launched the cutter in the Chipola River, along with some canoes they evidently found and confiscated. For the next two days, they encountered and spoke with other sympathetic Union folks and took aboard an escaped slave to serve as a guide. Assisted by the slave, they patrolled the area between January 20-24 for the steamer they believed was working the river in this area, but did not find the steamer. During this effort, they surprised a young slave girl, whom they thought would reveal their presence to Confederate forces in the area. They thus altered their mission and captured a few rebel troops garrisoned in the area, including one lieutenant, one sergeant, three privates, ten horses and various small arms, along with taking a number of escaped slaves. They also captured the residents of some adjacent homes who were sympathetic to the southern cause and who would have revealed their mission to local Confederate forces. Along the way, they also took possession of additional escaped slaves and burned a large "government warehouse" loaded with corn. Heading down the Chipola and Apalachicola Rivers, they arrived back at the USS *Midnight* in Apalachicola Bay on January 28. Similar to McCauley's boat raids on the Gulf coast (Chapter 6), this was a "high endurance" expedition that the sailors and marines performed brilliantly.

On May 31, 1865, Union Army forces with the 161st New York Infantry Regiment and the 82nd USCT (African American troops) permanently occupied Apalachicola, which had been intermittently occupied several other times prior to this, very similar to Jacksonville. The Army forces took possession of 944 bales of cotton, 868 of which had already been confiscated by naval authorities. The Army landing was supported by the gunboat USS *Itasca*, under Lt. Commander N. Green, which was one of the "90-day" gunboats.

In early March 1865, Union Gen. John Newton wanted to conduct an invasion into northern Florida to disrupt the small Confederate military units operating in the area and to move on Tallahassee, the state capitol. On March 3-4, 1865, a large flotilla of Union transports, carrying Army troops, supported by USN gunboats, hove to off the St. Marks River mouth. Ship's boats began to land the Army forces. Fog, heavy weather, and low tides that impeded crossing of the bar at the mouth of the river, all conspired to delay operations, but by March 5, the troops were all landed and began to make their way toward a railroad bridge over the St. Marks River, which they needed to cross to move on Tallahassee. The rebels succeeded in burning this structure, forcing the Union force to head towards a "natural bridge" where the St. Marks River went underground for a short distance before re-emerging at a river rise spring. The Union force was met at this location by a rag-tag Confederate defense consisting of militia (many elderly men), soldiers on leave and cadets from the nearby West Florida Seminary (current-day Florida State University), supported by a few small pieces of field artillery. The determined rebel force turned back the Union advance in what became known as the "Battle of Natural Bridge," the second major battle to be fought in Florida, after Olustee, and also a Union defeat.

At the conclusion of the war, Confederate Navy Secretary Mallory was arrested, as he tried to flee the country, and imprisoned for "treason." No trial of any kind was conducted, and in March 1866, President Andrew Johnson granted Mallory a parole, releasing him from jail. Eventually, he was allowed to return to Florida, where he

Map showing disposition of U.S. Navy vessels during the landing of troops at St. Marks. From the Official Records of the Union and Confederate Navies in the War of the Rebellion.

settled in Pensacola (his home before the war). Per the terms of his parole, he was no longer permitted to hold public office, but he made a decent living by resuming his law practice. His health gradually began to fail and he died in November 1873. He is buried in St. Michael's Cemetery in Pensacola, Florida.

Grave site of C.S. Navy Secretary Stephen R. Mallory in Pensacola. Photo by Tiffany Trent, used by permission.

South Florida

Blockade duty could be very boring, very exciting, and very hazardous. One of the mysteries of the war was the loss of the schooner *Annie*, which we met in Chapter 6, on patrol along the Big Bend. During the latter part of the war, the *Annie* was shifted to the blockade of southwest Florida. During that time, she mysteriously disappeared. Acting Volunteer Lieutenant C.H. Rockwell of the USS *Hendrick Hudson* eventually found her:

> *On the morning of the 4th* (February 1865), *being off Charlotte Harbor, I ran in to ascertain if anything had been heard from the ill-fated schooner* Annie *and to get the mails from the* Restless. *I was there informed that the mast of a vessel had been seen off Cape Roman. Leav-*

ing Charlotte Harbor the same day, I ran as far as Malco Inlet [Marco Pass?] and anchored at midnight. On the 5th I again weighed anchor, and, with a smooth sea and very favorable circumstances, succeeded at 1 p.m. in discovering the mast referred to in 6 fathoms of water, Cape Roman bearing N.E. by N., distant about 10 miles. I immediately hauled the bow of this ship alongside the mast, and with such means as I possessed succeeded at 11 p.m. raising the wreck sufficiently to bring her bow out of the water and identify her as the Annie, and discovered her condition. The catastrophe by which she was wrecked is still a mystery, and unless her crew have been saved I fear must remain so. From her foremast aft her deck is entirely gone, with the exception of the port side of the trunk cabin aft. From just abaft the fore rigging, on the starboard side, she is entirely gone - deck,

Steam gunboat USS *Hendrick Hudson*. Naval History and Heritage Command.

bottom, timbers, and everything from the keel out being completely cut off, with the exception of two or three of her floor timbers.

No vestige of her mainmast or the sail could be discovered, not even the stump. The pole of the maintopmast was found fast to the jib stay, the pennant halyards being wound around it with the toggle and head of the pennant. On the port side, from the fore rigging aft, *her rail was entirely gone, but I think her plank-sheer was whole on that side as far as the cabin. A more complete wreck could scarcely be imagined. Everything that could be found was saved. . . . With the grapnels and other appliances the whole hull was felt over to ascertain if any of the bodies of the crew could be discovered, but nothing was found except some clothing and bedding. Nothing could be found to throw any light on the manner of her loss. As I discovered her no vessel could have run her down and injure her to the extent seen by a single blow, although much may have washed off from her since her loss. From all I could see I think she must have been blown up, and can account for it in no other way.*

In the last year of the war, the intrepid Acting Lt. W.R. Browne was in command of the U.S. Bark *Pursuit*, patrolling off the Indian River on the east coast of Florida. The morning of March 16, 1865, Browne's lookouts sighted a schooner off the Indian River. They captured the British schooner *Mary*, out of the Bahamas. The schooner's cargo was rather pitiful, consisting of a box of shoes, a barrel of rum, and a box with a "large quantity of percussion caps." The prize and its crew were sent to Key West for adjudication.

As the war's end neared, Adm. Bailey had to step down as commander of the East Gulf Blockading squadron due to failing health. He was ultimately replaced by Acting Rear Adm. C.K. Stribling. U.S. Army Gen. Woodbury, who had an excellent working relationship with Bailey, died of yellow fever and was replaced by Gen. John Newton. Bailey and Woodbury had tried exceptionally hard to develop a good working relationship with the Florida Unionists, and were supportive and instrumental in helping them organize the resistance units and escaped slaves into military units. Adm. Stribling and Gen. Newton did not seem to appreciate the importance of this relationship, nor did they work well together (as Bailey and Woodbury did), and relations between the U.S. Army, Navy and the local Unionists began to deteriorate towards the end of the war.

Towards the very end of the war, the East Gulf Blockading Squadron headquarters in Key West received a terrifying piece of intelligence. In May 1865, the ocean-going ironclad ram CSS *Stonewall* put in to the port at Havana, Cuba. Built for the Confederate Navy by France, the *Stonewall* was a true sea-going ironclad warship and was immensely powerful. Steam-powered, she was heavily armored, had a huge fortified ram on the bow, and was armed with a

Navy barracks at Key West after the war. State Archives of Florida, Florida Memory Project.

massive 300-pdr Armstrong gun and two 70-pdr Armstrong guns. The U.S. Navy warships USS *Niagara* and USS *Sacramento* made weak attempts to confront her in March as she left Europe, but had generally avoided action with the formidable rebel warship. The U.S. Navy had nothing that could go up against this ship. Adm. Stribling wrote to Sec. Welles:

> *I have a dispatch this morning from the consul-general at Havana informing me that the* Stonewall *arrived there yesterday morning and that it was reported that she would leave to-day for Galveston. It is difficult to say what would be the result if she comes here unless the fort could stop her. I fear we could not successfully resist her.*

Stribling sent the USS *Powhatan* (with his flag captain aboard) and *Aries*, followed by the USS *Mahaska* and *Tallapoosa*, to blockade the harbor at Havana outside of the country's territorial zone (in international waters) with orders to engage the *Stonewall* should she try to make a run out of the harbor. Without consulting his superiors, Stribling sent a dispatch to the U.S. consul-general in Havana, to be delivered to the commander of the *Stonewall*:

> SIR: If the officers of the *Stonewall* are sensible men, they must be aware of the desperate state of the rebel cause and may be disposed to surrender the vessel if the officers and crew can be paroled on the same terms that Lee and others surrendered their armies. You will, therefore, in such manner as you may think best, let it be known that upon the surrender of the *Stonewall* to Commander Werden, commanding the *Powhatan*, and fleet captain (who is authorized to receive the surrender), with her armament and all public property, the officers and crew will be paroled on the same terms as were granted to General Lee and his army-the officers to retain their side arms and officers and men to retain their private effects. And to put them on an equality with Lee's army, I will send them to such port as may be agreed upon.
>
> There may be some rebel navy officers at Havana not belonging to the *Stonewall*, and as they may have influence, or even control, over her commander, they will, if they desire it, be included in the agreement and have the same privilege of retaining personal effects and being landed at the same place as the officers and crew of the *Stonewall*.
>
> It is needless for me to say anything further, as it must be evident to the commander of the *Stonewall* that he can not hope to make captures and carry them into any port for their benefit. If they can not do this there is no other means of support, and whatever means they may now have will soon be exhausted. If they surrender now, whatever private means they have will be saved.

Stribling also sent a dispatch to the Captain-General of Cuba (the official representative of the Spanish government ruling the island) informing him that, due to the collapse of the Confederate government, the *Stonewall* could no longer be considered a ship belonging to a legitimate, belligerent power (which enjoyed certain

Confederate sea-going ironclad CSS *Stonewall*. Naval History and Heritage Command.

protections under international law) and would therefore be considered a pirate. To provide shelter to this ship would be aiding and abetting piracy, authorizing the U.S. government to take whatever action necessary against the Island of Cuba. Stribling's communiqués were evidently persuasive enough. On May 21, 1865, he received a dispatch from the Captain-General of Cuba informing him that the *Stonewall* had been surrendered to Spanish naval authorities on May 19, and that the officers and crew had left the vessel and were paid off in Spanish gold. The warship was eventually turned over to the U.S. Navy, who sold it to Japan.

West Florida

Blockade running continued throughout the war, even "to the bitter end." In January 1865, the armed steamer USS *Honeysuckle* was on blockade off Cedar Key. A local Unionist informed Acting Master James J. Russell that he had been approached by some men asking if he would pilot their schooner into the Suwannee River. They represented themselves as U.S. Navy personnel. Russell dispatched two ship's boats under the command of Acting Ensign Charles N. Hall and Acting Third Assistant Engineer Charles E. Taber. After a long pull of seven hours, the boats found a schooner lying off the mouth of the West Pass of the Suwannee. They captured the schooner *Augusta*, of English registry, on January 17, carrying a cargo of lead, flour, cloth and coffee. The crew admitted to the bluejackets that they were trying to run the blockade.

About a week later, on January 23, the schooner *Fox* captured the schooner *Fannie McRae* off Warrior River, north of Deadman's Bay. And on March 3, 1865, the *Honeysuckle* off Cedar Key captured the sloop *Phantom* trying to make a run through the blockade into the Suwannee River (which the crew admitted to the sailors they were trying to do). The runner carried " . . .about 3,000 pounds of bar iron and a quantity of liquors."

Because the U.S. government had ordered their arrest, CSA President Jefferson Davis and his cabinet tried to flee the country at the end of the war in 1865. They headed south to the Florida coast, hoping to catch a blockade runner out of St. Marks and make their way to Texas or perhaps Mexico, where they could continue the war effort. Union Army units were alerted to this, and Davis was captured in Georgia on May 10, 1865. He was imprisoned for two years in Fort Monroe in Virginia, until he was released and allowed to return to the south, where he spent the remainder of his years trying to justify the

Drawing of the Gamble Mansion, near Ellenton. State Archives of Florida, Florida Memory Project.

Confederate cause. Confederate Secretary of State Judah P. Benjamin did manage to flee the country to England, where he lived the rest of his life. He escaped through Florida, and had taken up hiding for a short period of time in the Gamble Mansion in Manatee County, Florida, south of Tampa. John C. Breckinridge, who had served the Confederacy as a soldier and as its Secretary of War, also managed to flee the country through Florida, aided by Capt. John J. Dickison and his troopers.

The Role of the Navy in Florida

Scholars of Civil War history have debated how big a part the U.S. Navy's blockade played in bringing about overall Union victory in the Civil War. The debate has ranged at the extremes from "the Navy had nothing to do with it" to "the Navy won the war." Scholarly consensus appears to be that the naval blockade was a very important part of the overall Union war effort and that it contributed to the shortening of the war, which was one of his initial objectives when Army Gen. Winfield Scott first proposed a naval blockade of the southern coast.

The role and importance of the Navy blockade in Florida I think is more clearly evident; they were a vital part of the Union war effort here in Florida. The firepower of U.S. Navy gunboats on the coast and in the rivers was a big deterrent to Confederate military action against Union forces in the state. Although Confederate Gen. Braxton Bragg had assembled a force of 8,000 troops at Pensacola (and the same number nearby as reinforcements) to attempt an assault on Fort Pickens, the heavy armament of the U.S. Navy ships supporting the fort was a big factor in dissuading him from this effort. Along the St. Johns River, the constant presence of USN gunboats provided fire support for many Union Army movements along the river. Confederate Gen. P.G.T. Beauregard was hesitant to make a push on the Union forces at Jacksonville after the Battle of Olustee because of the presence of the naval gunnery. The words of the New Orleans Daily Delta after the Battle of Shiloh seem particularly relevant to the role of the U.S. Navy in Florida:

> *It* (The battle at Shiloh) *has taught us that we have nothing to fear from a land invasion of the enemy if he is unsupported by his naval armaments. It has taught us that the right arm of his power in this war is in his gun-*

> boats on our seacoast; and that our only assurance of saving the Mississippi from his grasp is to paralyze that arm upon its waters.

In addition to the blockade, the numerous naval shore party raids to capture and/or destroy blockade runners, destroy salt works and other manufacturing facilities, capture cotton, naval stores or lumber, and carry off escaping slaves, were a major blow to the Florida economy. This was especially true during the latter half of the war, when the state's importance to the Confederacy was magnified. Historians William Nulty, Nick Wynne and Joe Crankshaw have noted that while these USN actions in Florida were all minor events, individually each of which was insignificant from the perspective of the wider war effort, collectively the shore raid activities of the Florida blockade crippled the state, with ripple effects throughout the rest of the Confederate economy.

One of the major contributions of the U.S. Navy in the blockade of Florida was supporting and organizing the relatively large number of Union sympathizers in the state and aiding and abetting the freeing of slaves. The East Gulf Blockading squadron was the most active squadron in this regard, responsible for organizing a company of white cavalry, the 2nd Florida Cavalry, U.S., and a regiment of African American troops, the 2nd Regiment USCT. George Buker believes that this was the major accomplishment of this squadron; a feat he believes is overlooked by many historians. The 2nd Cavalry conducted extensive guerilla raids and expeditions into the interior, disrupting the southern economy. The 2nd Regiment USCT conducted military operations along the southwest Florida coast up to Tampa Bay, and was involved in the landing at St. Marks in 1865. They frequently worked in conjunction with the 2nd Cavalry, some of whom eventually grew to respect the black soldiers' abilities.

Interestingly, Buker notes that the ships and men of the South Atlantic Squadron had equal amounts of contact and interaction with Unionist Floridians and slaves along the northeast coast of the state (Chapter 4), but failed to capitalize on the potential of this resource. He feels that if the South Atlantic Squadron had been as active at organizing Floridians militarily as the East Gulf Squadron, they may have helped turn the tide at Olustee, by operating in the rear and disrupting the flow of Confederate supplies to their armies there. They could also have supplemented Union actions in this region in numerous other valuable ways.

The Civil War represented the maturation of what is today termed "joint operations," the cooperative actions of multiple service branches. Although some small-scale joint operations were conducted during the Mexican War, and earlier during the Seminole Wars, it was in the Civil War that joint actions became a significant part of strategic warfare for the U.S. On a national level, joint Army/Navy actions were responsible for many of the great victories of the war: the taking of Hatteras Inlet, Port Royal and Ft. Pulaski, and the conquest of the Mississippi (including the taking of New Orleans and Vicksburg). This cooperation was no less important for the war in Florida, and was seen in the retaking of Ft. Clinch and occupation of Fernandina, the occupation of Jacksonville, the taking of the battery at St. Johns Bluff, and actions on the Gulf coast.

Did the U.S. Navy help with the restoration of Florida to the Union? That is a question I think history scholars are better able to answer, but it is worth noting the largely non-hostile attitude the Navy displayed towards the civilian populace of the state throughout the war. Time and again, USN personnel provided support and aid to sympathetic Unionist civilians, and even to those who displayed no hostility towards the sailors, but were not necessarily Unionists. The Navy only targeted military assets, or civilian assets that contributed to the southern war effort (e.g., salt works, blockade running ships, etc.). In most sectors of their operation, Florida citizens came to view the Union Navy as a trusted friend as the war dragged on and their lives deteriorated. The U.S. Navy provided shelter for civilian refugees at Fernandina, Mayport Mills, St. Augustine, Key West, Southwest Florida, Egmont Key, Seahorse Key and Pensacola and aboard their gunboats.

Scholars of Civil War naval history give tremendous credit to C.S. Navy Secretary Stephen Mallory for putting together a credible Navy literally from scratch. What would have happened if the Confederate Navy had more of a presence in Florida during the war? Could they have supported southern troop movements similar to what the U.S. Navy did for the north?

If Mallory had been able to get one or more ironclads to the Florida coast, could they have had their way with the USN blockading fleets of wooden vessels, as the CSS *Virginia* did with the North Atlantic Squadron on March 8, 1862? At the end of the war, the Confederates were very close to completing the ironclad CSS *Jackson* in Columbus, Georgia. This was a very formidable warship, which was specifically designed to sortie down the Chattahoochee/Apalachicola Rivers, clear the shallow bar at high tide, and break the blockade of Apalachicola. The *Jackson* was destroyed at the end of the war to prevent its capture. Adm. Buchanan in Mobile, Alabama, considered taking his ironclad CSS *Tennessee* to Pensacola early in 1864 to try to retake that port. What if he had been able to do this, in conjunction with a successful effort by the *Jackson*?

What would have happened if the rebel gunboat CSS *Chattahoochee* had not blown up and was able to confront the activities of the blockaders on the Apalachicola River and thwart their efforts?

If the CSS *Stonewall* had been able to make it to the U.S. coast earlier, could it have turned the tide of the war for the Confederacy?

These are questions we will never be able to answer, but it is fun to think about. It seems to me that if the C.S. Navy had been able to devote resources to the Florida theatre, they may have enjoyed considerable success, with prospects for their overall war effort.

Remains of the wooden hull of the CSS *Jackson* at the Port Columbus Civil War Naval Museum. The metal framework over the hull shows the dimensions of the ironclad casemate. Author's photo.

Final Thoughts on the Navy in the Civil War in Florida

While the unprecedented bloodshed, carnage and suffering that occurred in combat during the Civil War gives thoughtful persons pause to this day, much attention has been focused on the casualties sustained by the great armies of the North and South as they fought on land. This is certainly justified based on the shear numbers involved in those engagements.

We don't think about this as much, but Union and Confederate sailors and marines also fought and died during the war in Florida and elsewhere, albeit not at the scale of the armies. Yet it should be of some note that the first Union combat deaths in the Civil War in Florida were Navy men, during the raid on the privateer *Judah* in Pensacola Bay in September 1861 (Chapter 3). I have held off mention of these men's names until here, because I think they deserve special note: they were Boatswain's Mate Charles M. Lamphere, Seaman John R. Herring (captain of a boat howitzer), and Marine Private John Smith. In the face of this tragedy, it seems oddly fitting that both sailors and a marine were among these first three deaths, indicating the close brotherhood of the two services that has existed throughout their history.

In this book, I have tried to highlight the efforts of the Confederate and Union Navy "tars," the Marine privates, and the non-commissioned and commissioned officers who led them. Maxine Turner in her book "Navy Gray" noted that the resourcefulness of the Confederate Navy to build and outfit gunboats in Georgia to try to break the blockade at Apalachicola was a marvel of logistics. Union sailors and marines died in combat in Florida, while working with energy, determination and just plain sweat to implement the blockade and conduct shore raids to disrupt the southern economy. Although their deaths did not number in the thousands, they all certainly still matter to this day. Viewing the graves of Seamen Patrick Doran and John Bishop on Seahorse Key brings home the sacrifices made by Navy men during the war. We have seen that one Marine Sgt. was awarded the Medal of Honor for bravery in combat during the Civil War in Florida; Marine Sgt. Nugent of the USS *Fort Henry*. He exemplifies the spirit of the men who served on the blockade of the Florida coast. While there may always be debate about the overall role of the Union Navy in the entire war effort, I don't think there would be any debate that the Union Navy helped win the war in Florida.

Appendix 1. Warships of the Florida Blockade

I put this list together by consulting the Squadron Reports in the "Official Records of the Union and Confederate Navies," indicating "Disposition of vessels of the South Atlantic/East Gulf/West Gulf Squadrons" issued at the end of each year 1861-1864 and the period May-June 1865. I picked the end-of-year reports under the assumption that ships on station at the end of the year would have been those who had been at least some portion of the year on that patrol, and were not new arrivals. I spot-checked this by randomly consulting mid-year reports 1862-64. I did not include Army transport ships, which mainly served to ferry troops and equipment about and rarely engaged in blockade operations. This list just shows commissioned warships and gunboats that served on blockade off Florida at some point during the war. If a ship served in two squadrons, I listed it in both. Most of the ship information is from the "Dictionary of American Naval Fighting Ships" on the Naval History and Heritage Command web site at: http://www.history.navy.mil/danfs/index.html.

** = captured blockade runner converted to U.S. Navy gunboat.

South Atlantic Blockading Squadron

Ship Name	Type	Dimensions	Armament
Bienville	Side-wheel steamer	1,558 tons; 253' length; 38' beam	8 32-pdr smoothbore guns; 1 30-pdr rifle
Braziliera	Sailing bark	541 tons; 135'8" length; 28'7" beam	6 32-pdr smoothbore guns
Cimarron	Side-wheel steamer	860 tons; 205' length; 35' beam	1 100-pdr rifle; 1 9" smoothbore; 6 24-pdr smoothbore howitzers
Columbine	Steam tug	133 tons; 117' length; 36' beam	2 20-pdr rifles
Dai Ching	Screw-steamer	520 tons; 170'6" length; 29'4" beam	4 24-pdr smoothbore; 2 20-pdr rifles; 1 100-pdr rifle
Darlington**	Side-wheel steamer	300 tons	1 boat howitzer
E. B. Hale	Screw-steamer	220 tons; 117' length; 28' beam	4 32-pdr guns

Ellen	Side-wheel steamer (ferryboat)	341 tons; 125' length; 28' beam	2 32-pdr guns; 2 30-pdr rifles
Fernandina	Sailing bark	297 tons; 115' length; 29' beam	6 32-pdr guns
Flambeau	Scew-steamer	850 tons; 180' length; 30' beam	1 30-pdr rifle; 1 20-pdr rifle
Gem of the Sea	Sailing bark	371 tons; 116' length; 26'3" beam	6 32-pdr guns
Henry Andrew	Screw-steamer	177 tons; 150' length; 26' beam	2 32-pdr guns; 1 20-pdr gun
Huntsville	Screw-steamer	860 tons; 196'4" length; 29'6" beam	1 unspecified caliber gun; 2 32-pdr guns
Huron	*Unadilla*-Class gunboat	507 tons; 158' length; 28' beam	1 XI-in Dahlgren smoothbore gun; 1 20-pdr Parrott rifle; 2 24-pdr howitzers
Isaac Smith	Screw-steamer	453 tons; 171'6" length; 31'4" beam	1 30-pdr Parrott rifle; 8 VIII-in Dahlgren smoothbores
Keystone State	Side-wheel steamer	1,364 tons; 220' length; 35' beam	4 12-pdr guns (howitzers)
Midnight	Sailing bark	387 tons; 126' length; 27'10" beam	6 32-pdr smoothbore guns; 1 20-pdr Parrott rifle
Mohawk	Screw-steamer	464 tons; 162'4" length; 24'4" beam	4 32-pdr guns
Mohican	Steam sloop-of-war	1,461 tons; 198'9" length; 33' beam	2 XI-inch Dahgren guns; 4 32-pdr guns
Norwich	Screw-steamer	450 tons; 132'5" length; 24'6" beam	1 30-pdr Parrott rifle; 4 8-in guns
Ottawa	*Unadilla*-Class gunboat	691 tons; 158'4" length; 28' beam	1 XI-in Dahlgren smoothbore gun; 1 20-pdr Parrott rifle; 2 24-pdr guns
Para	Sailing schooner	200 tons; 98' length; 24' beam	2 32-pdr guns
Patroon	Screw-steamer	183 tons; 113' length; 22'5" beam	1 30-pdr Parrott rifle; 4 8" guns

Paul Jones	Side-wheel steamer	1,210 tons; 216'10" length; 35'4" beam	1 100-pdr rifle; 2 11" guns; 2 50-pdr guns; 2 24-pdr guns
Pawnee	Steam-screw gunboat	1,533 tons; 221'6" length; 47' beam	8 9-in guns; 2 12-pdr guns
Pembina	*Unadilla*-Class gunboat	507 tons; 171' length; 31'6" beam	1 XI-in Dahlgren smoothbore gun; 1 20-pdr Parrott rifle; 2 24-pdr guns
Penguin	Screw-steamer	389 tons; 155' length; 30'8" beam	4 32-pdr guns; 1 12-pdr gun
Perry	Sailing brig	280 tons; 105' length; 25'6" beam	2 32-pdr guns; 6 32-pdr carronades
Pocahontas	Screw-steamer	558 tons; 169'6" length; 26'3" beam	4 32-pdr guns; 1 10-pdr; 1 20-pdr Parrott rifle
Potomska	Screw-steamer/schooner	287 tons; 134'6" length; 27' beam	4 32-pdr guns; 1 20-pdr Parrott rifle
Seneca	*Unadilla*-Class gunboat	507 tons; 158'4" length; 28' beam	1 XI-in Dahlgren smoothbore gun; 1 20-pdr Parrott rifle; 2 24-pdr howitzers
Unadilla	*Unadilla*-Class gunboat	507 tons; 158' length; 28' beam	1 XI-in Dahlgren smoothbore gun; 1 20-pdr Parrott rifle; 2 24-pdr howitzers
Uncas	Screw-steamer	192 tons; 118'6" length; 23'4" beam	1 20-pdr Parrott rifle; 2 32-pdr guns
Wabash	Steam-screw frigate	4,808 tons; 301'6' length; 51'4" beam	2 X-in Dahlgren smoothbore guns; 14 VIII-in Dahlgren smoothbore guns ; 24 IX-in Dahlgren smoothbore guns
Water Witch	Side-wheel steamer	378 tons; 150' length; 23' beam	4 32-pdr guns

East Gulf Blockading Squadron

Ship Name	Type	Dimensions	Armament
*Adela***	Side-wheel steamer	585 tons; 211' length; 23'6" beam	2 20-pdr Parrott Rifles; 4 24-pdr smoothbore guns
Amanda	Sailing bark	368 tons; 117'6" length; 27'9" beam	6 32-pdr smoothbore guns
*Annie***	Sailing schooner	27 tons; 46'2" length; 14' beam	1 12-pdr smoothbore howitzer
*Ariel***	Sailing schooner	20 tons;	1 12-pdr smoothbore gun
*Aries***	Screw-steamer	820 tons; 201' length; 27'10" beam	4 8-in smoothbore guns; 1 30-pdr Parrot rifle; 1 12-pdr rifle
*Beauregard***	Sailing schooner	10 tons;	1 30-pdr rifle; 2 12-pdr boat howitzers
*Britannia***	Side-wheel steamer	495 tons; 189' length; 26' beam	1 30-pdr Parrot rifle; 12 12-pdr rifles; 2 24-pdr howitzers
*Clyde***	Side-wheel steamer	294 tons; 200'6" length; 18'6" beam	2 24-pdr boat howitzers
Crusader	Screw-steamer	545 tons; 169' length; 28' beam	4 32-pdr guns; 8 24-pdr guns; 1 12-pdr howitzer
Dale	Sailing sloop	566 tons; 117' length; 32' beam	14 32-pdr guns; 2 12-pdr guns
Ethan Allen	Sailing bark	556 tons; 153'6" length; 35'1" beam	6 32-pdr guns
Eugenie	Sailing schooner	150 tons; (other data not provided)	"1 gun" – no specifics
Fort Henry	Side-wheel steamer (ferryboat)	519 tons; 150'6" length; 32' beam	2 IX-in Dahlgren guns; 4 32-pdr smoothbore guns
*Fox***	Sailing schooner	80 tons;	1 12-pdr rifle; 1 12-pdr smoothbore
Gem of the Sea	Sailing bark	371 tons; 116' length; 26'3" beam	6 32-pdr guns

Hatteras	Side-wheel steamer	1,126 tons; 210' length	4 32-pdr guns; 1 20-pdr gun
Hendrick Hudson**	Screw-steamer	460 tons; 171' length; 29'11" beam	4 8-inch guns; 2 20-pdr guns
Hibiscus	Screw-steamer	490 tons; no other data	2 30-pdr guns; 4 24-pdr guns
Honduras	Side-wheel steamer	376 tons; 150' length; 27' beam	2 12-pdr rifled guns
Honeysuckle	Steam tug	241 tons; 123' length; 20'2" beam	2 20-pdr guns
Huntsville	Screw-steamer	860 tons; 196'4" length; 29'6" beam	1 unspecified caliber gun; 2 32-pdr guns
Ino	Sailing ship	895 tons; 160'6" length; 34'11" beam	8 32-pdr guns
Isonomia	Side-wheel steamer	593 tons; 212' length; 30' beam	1 3 (?)-pdr Parrott rifle; 2 24-pdr boat howitzers
Itasca	Unadilla-Class gunboat	507 tons; 158' length; 28' beam	1 X-in Dahlgren smoothbore gun; 1 20-pdr Parrott rifle; 2 32-pdr guns
Iuka	Side-wheel steamer	944 tons; 200' length	1 20-pdr Parrott rifle; 1 heavy & 1 light 12-pdr boat howitzer; 1 24-pdr boat howitzer
James S. Chambers	Sailing schooner	401 tons; 124'6" length; 29'3" beam	4 32-pdr guns
James L. Davis	Sailing bark	461 tons; 133' length; 30'7" beam	4 8-inch guns
Julia**	Sailing schooner	10 tons;	No-information
Kingfisher	Sailing bark	451 tons; 121'4" length; 28'8" beam	4 VIII-in Dahlgren guns
Magnolia**	Side-wheel steamer	843 tons;	1 20-pdr Parrott rifle; 4 24-pdr guns (howitzers probably)

Mahaska	Side-wheel steamer	1,070 tons; 228'2" length; 33'10" beam	1 100-pdr Parrott rifle; 1 9-in gun; 4 24-pdr guns
Marigold	Steam tug	115 tons; 84'7" length; 18'9" beam	1 12-pdr howitzer; 1 12-pdr rifled howitzer
Marion	Sailing sloop-of-war	566 tons; 117' length; 32' beam	16 guns (unspecified)
Matthew Vassar	Sailing schooner	216 tons; 93'7" length; 27'2" beam	1 13" mortar; 2 32-pdr guns
Mercedita	Screw-steamer	1,000 tons; 183'6" length; 30'3" beam	8 32-pdr guns
Midnight	Sailing bark	387 tons; 126' length; 27'10" beam	1 20-pdr Parrott rifle; 6 32-pdr guns
Mohawk	Screw-steamer	464 tons; 162'4" length; 24'4" beam	4 32-pdr guns
Montgomery	Screw-steamer	787 tons; 201'6" length' 28'7" beam	4 32-pdr guns
Nita**	Side-wheel steamer	210 tons; 146' length; 22'4" beam	2 heavy 12-pdr smoothbores; 1 12-pdr howitzer
O. H. Lee	Sailing schooner	No data	No data
Oleander	Side-wheel steamer	246 tons; 143' length; 22'6" beam	2 20-pdr Parrott rifles
Penguin	Screw steamer	389 tons; 155' length; 30'8" beam	4 32-pdr guns; 1 12-pdr gun (howitzer?)
Port Royal	Side-wheel steamer	805 tons; 209' length; 35' beam	No-information
Powhatan	Side-wheel steamer	2,415 tons; 253'8" length; 45' beam	1 XI-in Dahlgren gun; 10 IX-in Dahlgren guns; 5 12-pdr guns
Proteus	Screw-steamer	1,244 tons; 203' length; 36' beam	1 100-pdr Parrot rifle; 2 30-pdr Parrot rifles; 6 32-pdr guns; 2 12-pdr rifles (howitzers?)

Pursuit	Sailing bark	600 tons; 144' length; 34'10" beam	6 32-pdr guns
R. R. Cuyler	Screw-steamer	1,200 tons; 237' length; 33'3" beam	8 32-pdr guns; 2 rifles
Restless	Sailing bark	265 tons; 108'8" length; 27'8" beam	4 32-pdr guns
Roebuck	Sailing bark	455 tons; 135' length; 27' beam	4 32-pdr guns
*Rosalie***	Sailing sloop	28 tons; 45' length; 17' beam	1 12-pdr howitzer
St. Lawrence	Sailing frigate	1,726 tons; 175' length; 45' beam	8 8-inch shell guns; 42 32-pdr guns
Sagamore	*Unadilla*-Class gunboat	507 tons; 158' length; 28' beam	1 20-pdr gun; 2 24-pdr guns; 1 light 12-pdr gun (howitzer)
San Jacinto	Steam-screw frigate	1,567 tons'; 234' length; 37'9" beam	2 8-inch guns; 4 32-pdr guns
Sea Bird	Sailing schooner	58 tons; 59'8" length'; 18'4" beam	1 12-pdr boat howitzer
Somerset	Side-wheel steamer (ferry-boat)	521 tons; 151' length; 32'4" beam	2 IX-in Dahlgren guns; 4 32-pdr smoothbore guns
Spirea	Side-wheel steamer	409 tons;	2 30-pdr Parrott rifles; 4 24-pdr smoothbore howitzers
Stars and Stripes	Screw-steamer	407 tons; 124'3" length; 34'6" beam	4 8-in guns; 1 20-pdr Parrott rifle.
*Stonewall***	Sailing Schooner	30 tons;	1 heavy 12-pdr smoothbore howitzer
Sunflower	Steam tug	294 tons; 104'5" length; 20'9" beam	2 30-pdr Parrott rifles

Ship Name	Type	Dimensions	Armament
Tahoma	Unadilla-Class gunboat	507 tons; 158'4" length; 28' beam	1 X-in Dahlgren smoothbore gun; 2 20-pdr Parrott rifles; 2 24-pdr howitzers
Tallapoosa	Side-wheel steamer	974 tons; 205' length; 35' beam	2 100-pdr Parrott rifles; 4 IX-in Dahlgren smoothbore guns; 2 20-pdr Parrott rifles; 2 24-pdr howitzers
Two Sisters**	Sailing schooner	54 tons;	1 12-pdr boat howitzer
Wanderer**	Sailing schooner	300 tons; 106' length; 25'6" beam	1 20-pdr Parrott rifle; 2 24-pdr boat howitzers
Yucca	Steam tug	373 tons; 145'7" length; 23'7" beam	1 30-pdr Parrott rifle; 1 12-pdr smoothbore howitzer

West Gulf Blockading Squadron

Ship Name	Type	Dimensions	Armament
Albatross	Screw-steamer/bark	378 tons; 150' length; 30' beam	1 VIII-in Dahlgren smoothbore gun; 2 32-pdr smoothbore guns
Arthur	Sailing bark	554 tons; 133' length; 31'2" beam	6 32-pdr smoothbore guns
Bloomer	Stern-wheel steamboat	130 tons	1 32-pdr gun; 1 12-pdr rifled howitzer
Bohio	Sailing brig	No data	No data
Brooklyn	Steam sloop-of-war	2,532, tons; 233' length; 43' beam	1 10" smoothbore gun; 20 9" smoothbore guns
Charlotte**	Sailing schooner	70 tons;	2 guns (unspecified)
Colorado	Steam-screw frigate	3,425 tons; 268'6" length; 52'6" beam	2 X-in Dahlgren guns; 24 IX-in Dahlgren guns; 14 VIII-in Dahlgren guns

Name	Type	Dimensions	Armament
Genesee	Side-wheel steamer	803 tons; 209' length; 34'11" beam	1 X-in Dahlgren gun; 1 100-pdr Parrott rifle; 6 24-pdr howitzers
Hartford	Steam sloop-of-war	2,900 tons; 225' length; 44' beam	20 IX-in Dahlgren smoothbore; 2 20-pdr Parrott rifles; 2 12-pdr guns
Houghton (actual name *A. Houghton*)	Sailing bark	326 tons; 113'4" length; 25'3" beam	2 32-pdr smoothbore guns
J. C. Kuhn	Sailing bark	888 tons; 153' length; 35' beam	4 32-pdr guns
Jasmine	Steam tug	120 tons; 79' length; 18'3" beam	1 20-pdr Parrott rifle; 1 12-pdr howitzer
Maria A. Wood	Sailing schooner	344 tons; 125' length; 28'6" beam	2 32-pdr guns
Niagara	Steam-screw frigate	5,540 tons; 328'10" length; 55' beam	12 XI-in Dahlgren guns
*Nightingale***	Sailing ship (clipper-type)	1,066 tons; 177' length; 36' beam	4 32-pdr guns
Pinola	*Unadilla*-Class gunboat	507 tons; 158' length; 28' beam	1 XI-in Dahlgren smoothbore gun; 1 20-pdr Parrott rifle; 2 24-pdr howitzers
Potomac	Sailing frigate	1,726 tons; 177'10" length; 46'2" beam	8 8-in guns; 42 32-pdr guns
Preble	Sailing sloop-of-war	566 tons; 117' length; 32' beam	16 32-pdr guns
Rachel Seaman	Sailing schooner	303 tons; 115' length; 30' beam	2 32-pdr guns
Richmond	Steam sloop-of-war	2,604 tons; 225' length; 42'6" beam	20 IX-in Dahlgren smoothbore guns; 1 80-pdr Dahlgren smoothbore gun; 1 30-pdr Parrott rifle
Sabine	Sailing frigate	1,726 tons; 202'6" length; 47' beam	44-50 unspecified guns
*Sam Houston***	Sailing schooner	66 tons;	1 heavy 12-pdr smoothbore howitzer

St. Louis	Sailing sloop-of-war	700 tons; 127' length; 33'9" beam	20 24-pdr smoothbore guns
Vincennes	Sailing sloop-of-war	700 tons; 127' length; 33'9" beam	18 guns (unspecified)
Wyandotte	Screw-steamer	464 tons; no other data	4 32-pdr guns; 1 24-pdr boat howitzer

Appendix 2. Places to visit and events to attend that cover the Civil War Navies in Florida

Two excellent overall sources listing Civil War sites to visit in Florida are:

Taylor, Paul. Discovering the Civil War in Florida. A Reader and Guide. Sarasota: Pineapple Press, 2001. Paul's focus is mainly on the activities of the Union and Confederate Armies, but at a number of these sites near the coast or on rivers, the Union Navy was an active participant as well.

The Florida Civil War Heritage Trail. A guidebook published by the Florida Association of Museums. Available for free download on the Florida Department of State web site at:
http://www.flheritage.com/preservation/trails/civilwar/index.cfm

I have basically culled these two sources to list here sites you can visit today where Union Navy forces or Confederate Navy or steamboats were present in Florida during the war. I have also listed events that I, and/or members of my living history group, the USS *Ft. Henry*, regularly participate in as Union Navy seamen and marines, or events where I know there will be other Civil War Navy and/or Marine Living History units participating. Many of these sites and events charge a modest entrance fee, which is an important source of revenue to help maintain and keep the site open to the public, or to keep the event going.

Panhandle Florida

The National Civil War Naval Museum at Port Columbus is located in Columbus Georgia. Although not a Florida site, it is an essential stop for anyone interested in the naval side of the war (both North and South). The museum houses the remains of the CSS *Chattahoochee*, which blew up and sank on the Apalachicola River. It also has a massive collection of artifacts and numerous displays covering Union and Confederate Navy ships and activities during the war, along with a full-size replica of the USS/CSS *Water Witch*, which you can board and tour. The web site is: http://portcolumbus.org/. There is a reasonable admission fee to the museum, which is very important in helping to support their activities, or you can join as a member through annual dues, which depending on your level of membership, gets you and others in for free.

Fort Pickens. Located in Gulf Islands National Seashore. Information on the National Park Service web site:
http://www.nps.gov/guis/planyourvisit/fort-pickens.htm

Fort Barrancas. Located on the mainland near the Naval Aviation Museum. Information on the National Park Service web site at:
http://www.nps.gov/guis/planyourvisit/fort-barrancas.htm

Pensacola Light Station. Located on the grounds of the Pensacola Naval Air Station, the lighthouse is open to the public. There is a fee to climb the tower, but it is not excessive. Website:
http://www.pensacolalighthouse.org/

St. Michael's Cemetery. Located in Pensacola (detailed location in The Florida Civil War Heritage Trail). Confederate Navy Secretary Stephen R. Mallory is buried here.

St. Andrews Bay salt works and St. Andrews skirmish historical markers are located near each other on West Beach Drive in Panama City. The salt works marker is in a small public park and features a replica of a small salt boiler. More exact location information can be found in the The Florida Civil War Heritage Trail publication.

EVENT. The "St. Andrews Bay Salt Works Raid" living history event is held each year usually on the second or third weekend in April at a site on the waterfront in downtown Panama City. The event features re-enactors portraying Union sailors and marines, Confederate home guard militia, and local civilians. Period camps showing how they lived are set up and lectures on salt making are offered throughout the weekend. Sailors and marines conduct drills, demonstrations and presentations, and the event features an amphibious beach landing and assault on a rebel salt works by armed marines and seamen on Saturday and Sunday. Information can be found generally a few months before the event at:
http://events.panamacity.com/events.php . There is no fee to attend this event.

St. Joseph's salt works historical marker. Located in the town of Port St. Joe, it commemorates the destruction of the rebel works by the bark USS *Kingfisher*. Detailed location information is in the The Florida Civil War Heritage Trail publication.

Apalachicola. The town still has a great "old Florida" look and feel. Some of the old brick cotton warehouses along the riverfront still stand and are being renovated to house shops and cafes, but still keep their historic character.

Apalachicola Maritime Museum. The museum is a "work in progress" (in their own words) and is located along the waterfront in historic Apalachicola. A second location will eventually also open in Chattahoochee. The museum will feature exhibits and displays portraying the total maritime history of Apalachicola, including the Civil War period. Information is at: http://www.ammfl.org/ .

EVENT. The Apalachicola Maritime Museum began a Civil War Living History weekend in May 2013, which will continue to be held annually. The event includes re-enactors portraying Union Navy and Marine personnel and their camps, providing demonstrations and presentations on the actions of Navy and Marines in the region during the Civil War. Check their web site for dates and information.

St. George Island Lighthouse. This is the former Cape St. George lighthouse, which toppled over in 2005, but was present during the war and de-activated by Confederate sympathizers. Dedicated volunteers helped salvage and clean many of the original bricks from the fallen tower, and the original construction plans for the light were obtained from the Library of Congress. Funded by donations and grants, the light was reconstructed in a park on St. George Island across the bay from the town of Eastpoint. There is a nominal admission fee to climb the lighthouse tower. The lighthouse web site is:

http://www.stgeorgelight.org/index.cfm/m/1/dn/Home%20Page/

Crooked River Lighthouse. Located just outside the Town of Carrabelle. The current steel frame structure was built after the war (1895); it replaced the former Dog Island Lighthouse, which was de-activated by the Confederates during the war and was destroyed by a storm in 1873. There is a nominal admission fee to climb the tower. From the top of the tower, you get a nice view of St. George Sound. Web site: http://www.crookedriverlighthouse.org/index.cfm

CSS *Chattahoochee* monument. Located in the Town of Chattachoochee, the monument lists the names of the Confederate sailors killed when the gunboat's boilers exploded during a steam-up procedure. Detailed location information is in The Florida Civil War Heritage Trail publication.

St. Marks Lighthouse. Located in the St. Marks National Wildlife Refuge. Even if you can't get in the lighthouse, there is a nice view of the Gulf of Mexico/Apalachee Bay from the grounds, and you can look out and imagine Union Navy gunboats prowling off the coast. Contact the refuge to find out about open-house dates at the lighthouse: http://www.fws.gov/saintmarks/overview.html

EVENT. The first weekend of March, the "Battle of Natural Bridge" is re-enacted at the Natural Bridge Battlefield Historic State Park. Union Marine and Navy are usually present, as they provided flanking cover for the Army units as they attempted to move north. Information on the park web site at:
http://www.floridastateparks.org/naturalbridge/default.cfm .

Northeast Florida

Fort Clinch. Located within Ft. Clinch State Park. There is an admission fee to the park and another fee to access the fort; both are modest. Volunteers portraying Union Army personnel are usually present the first weekend of each month to talk about the fort in the war. Information is at:
http://www.floridastateparks.org/fortclinch/default.cfm

EVENT. The first weekend in May the fort hosts a large Union garrison recalling the occupation of the fort and adjacent batteries by Union forces in 1862. Union soldiers, sailors and marines are present to demonstrate fort life and duties during the war. The second weekend in October the fort hosts a large Confederate garrison to commemorate the takeover of the fort for a period of time at the beginning of the war by Confederate forces. The usual fees pertaining to park admission and admission to the fort apply during this event. See the events page on the fort web site at:
http://www.floridastateparks.org/fortclinch/events.cfm

Amelia Island Lighthouse. It was extinguished by the Confederates in 1861. When Union forces took Fernandina and nearby Ft. Clinch in 1862, they also took possession of the lighthouse. The property is open on weekends (but the lighthouse itself is not) from 11:00 AM-2:00 PM, and the City of Fernandina Beach conducts tours to the lighthouse the first and third Wednesdays of each month. They open the tower for you to look in, but you cannot climb to the lantern, because there is no handrail on the steps! There is a nominal charge for the tour and they only occur if they get a minimum of 10 people for a tour. Information is on the Fernandina Beach web site:
http://www.fbfl.us/index.aspx?NID=474 .

Fernandina (now Fernandina Beach). The Town of Fernandina was occupied by Union forces in March 1862. The Amelia Island Museum of History on 3rd Street has exhibits on the history of the town, including during the Civil War. Information at www.ameliamuseum.org.

Fort Caroline National Monument. The Ft. Caroline National Monument, at the north end of Jacksonville in the Timucuan Ecological and Historic Preserve, covers several periods of Florida history dating back to establishment of a French colony near the mouth of the St. Johns River in the 1500s. The site includes a portion of St. Johns Bluff, where the Confederate earthworks and battery were constructed in summer 1862. Nearby this site is a small public park with the Ribault Monument; this park appears to be nearer to where the battery actually was and gives you a good feel for what the view may have been like for the rebel soldiers manning the earthworks. The folks at the National Monument can direct you to the Ribault site. The National Monument web site is: http://www.nps.gov/foca/index.htm .

EVENT. Typically on a weekend in October, the National Monument hosts a Civil War Living History event. Period camps with Union Army soldiers, medical personnel and engineers are set up and Union Navy re-enactors are present to discuss the activities of USN gunboats on the St. Johns River during the war. Demonstration of weapons firing are held throughout the weekend, including the firing of a replica U.S. Navy Dahlgren 12-pdr boat howitzer. Check the park web site for information. There is no fee to attend this event.

Yellow Bluff Fort Historic State Park. Yellow Bluff Fort is a Confederate earthworks constructed in summer of 1862 during the same time the earthworks and battery were constructed on the other side of the river downstream at St. Johns Bluff. The Yellow Bluff earthworks were abandoned when the St. Johns Bluff fortification was, as a large Union force moved to take the latter. There is no fee to access the site. Information is on the State Parks web site at: http://www.floridastateparks.org/yellowbluff/default.cfm .

Mandarin Museum, Jacksonville. Located in Walter Jones Historical Park, the museum sits on the St. Johns River close to where the steamers *Maple Leaf* and *Gen. Hunter* were sunk by Confederate torpedoes in 1864. The Museum has a display of artifacts recovered from the wreck of the *Maple Leaf* and a nice model of the Union transport. Information at: http://www.mandarinmuseum.net/

Jacksonville Maritime Heritage Center. A museum covering the maritime history of Jacksonville. Includes some artifacts and information on the Civil War Navy in Jacksonville. There is a nominal fee to gain access to the museum. Web site: http://www.jacksonvillemaritimeheritagecenter.org/ .

Jacksonville Museum of Science and History. Located in downtown Jacksonville, the museum features a number of artifacts recovered from the wreck of the *Maple Leaf*, along with other exhibits on the Civil War in Jacksonville. Information at: http://www.themosh.org/Home.html .

Castillo De San Marcos National Monument. Located in historic St. Augustine, this fort dates back to the Spanish colonial period, and was named Ft. Marion during the Civil War. The interpretive activities at the fort mainly emphasize the Spanish colonial and early American revolutionary periods, but they do occasionally have events that include Civil War living historians, including U.S. Navy personnel.

There is a nominal admission fee to the fort. Information at: http://www.nps.gov/casa/index.htm .

St. Augustine Light Station and Museum. Like so many others, the St. Augustine light was de-activated by the Confederates at the beginning of the war. The current tower was constructed after the war, in 1874, but another lighthouse was nearby during the war. There is a nominal admission fee that helps support the activities of the St. Augustine Lighthouse Association, who helps run the light. Information at: http://www.staugustinelighthouse.org/events/sea-your-history .

Columbine/Horse Landing mural. A mural depicting the USS *Columbine* on the St. Johns River and Confederate Capt. John J. Dickison and his men about to attack is on 3rd Street, south of St. Johns Avenue, in downtown Palatka.

EVENT. A Civil War Living History event is held on the grounds of the historic Bronson-Mulholland house in Palatka the last weekend of September. Re-enactors portraying Union Army infantry and engineers recall the "Occupation of Palatka" by Union forces in 1864. Union Navy re-enactors are also present at this event to discuss the activities of USN gunboats on the adjacent St. Johns River during the war. There is no fee to attend this event. Check the Putnam County Historical Society web site at: http://putnam-fl-historical-society.org/ .

Horse Landing historic marker. An historic marker noting the attack on and sinking of the USS *Columbine* is located on the grounds of the Rodeheaver Boys Ranch, south of Palatka on SR 19. This is a privately owned facility and you need to contact them to gain permission to enter the site and view the marker. Their phone # is (386) 328-1281.

Tampa Bay and the Big Bend

Ballast Point Historical Markers. Historical markers recalling the activities of blockade runners and Hillsborough River Raid/Battle of Ballast Point are located in Tampa. Detailed location information is in The Florida Civil War Heritage Trail publication.

Fort Brooke artillery pieces. Located in Plant Park on the grounds of the University of Tampa, two of the 24-pdr artillery pieces that were mounted in Ft. Brooke are displayed. These were recovered by Henry B. Plant when he was building his hotel (current-day University of Tampa) in 1891 and placed at this site.

EVENT. Egmont Key Open House. Usually held a weekend in November (mostly the second weekend), a ferry takes spectators out to visit Egmont Key, an important secondary base of operations for the East Gulf Blockading Squadron. Re-enactors from the USS *Ft. Henry* LHA are usually present on the Key during the event to discuss the activities of the U.S. Navy in the Tampa Bay area during the war. There is a fee for the ferry out to the Key. Information about the ferry is on the Ft. DeSoto Park web site at: http://www.pinellascounty.org/park/05_Ft_DeSoto.htm .

EVENT. The Brooksville Raid Re-enactment is held the third weekend of January on the grounds of the Sand Hill Boy Scout Camp near Weeki Wachee (outside of Brooksville, FL). The event recalls the raid made by a small Union Army force in July 1864. The USS *Ft. Henry* LHA usually has their biggest turnout at this event, with a full-scale naval landing party camp set-up and demonstrations, lectures and sea shanty music presented in camp throughout the weekend. A large battle between Union and Confederate forces is re-enacted both Saturday and Sunday (which does not simulate the actual raid). Information can be found at the event's Facebook page: https://www.facebook.com/brooksvillereenactment/page_map or at the Hernando Historical Museum Association web site at: http://hernandohistoricalmuseum.org/ . There is a nominal admission fee to attend/access this event, as it is an important fundraiser for the Boy Scout Camp.

EVENT. A living history event recalling the Hillsborough River Raid and the Battle of Ballast Point is held the last or next-to-last weekend of February at Ft. DeSoto County Park in southern Pinellas County. The event features period camps with Union and Confederate Army and Union Navy and Marine re-enactors conducting drills, demonstrations and presentations. A small skirmish representing a beach landing is fought on Saturday and Sunday. There is no fee to attend this event, but there is a small toll fee to access Ft. DeSoto Park on the Pinellas Bayway toll road. Google the event a few months prior to check for information or check with the park office at (727) 552-1862.

EVENT. Crystal River Boat Bash. Held usually in early April, this event spotlights small wooden boats hand-made with period carpentry tools, including yawls, skiffs, cutters, etc. The replica of the scow *Wartappo* is being built by this group and should be completed soon. Members of the USS *Ft. Henry* LHA are present to discuss the activities of Union Navy and Marine personnel in the Crystal River area during the war.

Cedar Key. Like Apalachicola, the Town of Cedar Key still has that "old-timey" Florida feel. Several structures in the town date back to the Civil War period, particularly the Island Hotel on 2nd Street near the public park, which may have been used as a Union barracks and storehouse during the latter part of the war when U.S. Army forces occupied the town. From the city dock, you can look out on the bay surrounding the keys and imagine U.S. Navy gunboats on blockade patrol.

Cedar Key Museum State Park. Located outside of town, the State Museum has displays that include information and artifacts about Cedar Key during the Civil War. A salt kettle used at a salt works is located on the grounds of the site. Information at: http://www.floridastateparks.org/cedarkeymuseum/default.cfm . There is a very small fee to enter the museum itself, but none to roam the grounds.

EVENT. An open house is held on Seahorse Key each month during weekend high tides when it is easier to access the site. The Key is normally closed to the public except for these weekends. Local water taxis provide transport out to the Key and back for a fee. The lighthouse can be visited and climbed and Union Navy and Marine re-enactors from the *Ft. Henry* try to be present at some of these events in October and December to discuss the activities of the U.S. Navy there during the Civil War. A small cemetery with the graves of three Union Navy seamen from the real USS *Ft. Henry* is on the Key. Check with the Refuge office for a schedule and more information about these open houses: lowersuwannee@fws.gov or (352) 493-0238.

Troy Springs State Park. Located on the Suwannee River outside of the Town of Mayo in Lafayette County, the remains of the Confederate steamboat *Madison* are in the spring run out to the river. The only thing remaining are the ribs of the hull. The steamboat was burned and sunk in 1863 by its owner/captain to prevent capture by Union forces. It represents the rebel steamboat activity on the Suwannee, Apalachicola, and other Florida rivers during the war. There is a small fee to enter the park. Information at: http://www.floridastateparks.org/troyspring/default.cfm .

City of Hawkinsville Underwater Archaeological Site. Access to this site is only via boat and it is a state-designated underwater archaeological preserve. It is located on the Suwannee River upstream of the Town of Fanning Springs, adjacent to an old railroad bridge crossing the river that is now part of the Nature Coast State Trail. The steamboat *City of Hawkinsville* was built after the war, but it is still a good example of what a Confederate steamboat plying the Suwannee River during the war might have looked like. Diving conditions on this wreck can be hazardous and it is not for novice divers. An interpretive panel on the wreck is located at the Wayside Park on the east side of the US 19 bridge over the Suwannee River. Information is also at the Florida Department of State web site at: http://www.museumsinthesea.com/hawkinsville/index.htm .

Taylor County salt works marker. An historic marker commemorating the salt-making activities in Taylor County during the war is located at the intersection of US 19 and County Road 361, south of Perry, FL on US 19.

South Florida

Ponce de Leon Inlet Light Station. The light station at Ponce Inlet (formerly Mosquito Inlet) was constructed after the war, and a lighthouse was not present here during the war. However, you can get a nice view of the Inlet and Mosquito Lagoon from the top of the lighthouse and can imagine Union blockade gunboats patrolling off the Inlet. Information is on their web site at: http://ponceinlet.org/ . There is a nominal fee to enter the site and climb the tower.

New Smyrna (now New Smyrna Beach). The town was actively used by blockade runners during the war. The New Smyrna Museum of History has displays of artifacts from the area during the Civil War. There is no entry fee, but donations are requested which help support the museum and its activities. Information at: http://www.nsbhistory.org/ .

Jupiter Inlet Lighthouse. The light was extinguished by the Confederates in 1861, but components and the fuel were discovered by Union raiders during the war. The lighthouse is still a U.S. Coast Guard-operated facility, but it is open to the public and you can climb the tower with a guided tour. You get a good view of Jupiter Inlet and the Indian River from the top of the tower. Web site: http://www.jupiterlighthouse.org/ . There is a nominal fee to participate in the guided climb of the tower.

Cape Florida Lighthouse. Located in Bill Baggs Cape Florida State Park. The lighthouse was the southern-most one on the Florida east coast that was extinguished by the Confederates in 1861. The keeper and assistant keeper had vowed to defend it from the rebels and keep it lit, but the two were routed by a Confederate raiding party from the Jupiter Inlet lighthouse. The lighthouse is open for tours and climbing when the park is open. Information at: http://www.floridastateparks.org/capeflorida/default.cfm . There is a nominal entrance fee to the park; I am not sure about fees to climb the tower.

Mallory home site historical marker. An historic marker in Clinton Square Park in Key West recognizes that nearby was the family home of Confederate Navy Secretary Stephen Mallory.

Remaining structures from the Key West Naval Base. Two structures in Key West are remnants of the U.S. Navy base there during the war; the Clinton Square Market at 291 Front Street was a USN coal storage and warehouse on the Navy base and the structure at 401 Emma Street was the U.S. Marine Hospital.

Fort Zachary Taylor Historic State Park. One of the forts continuously occupied by Union forces throughout the war. A Civil War living history event is usually held at this site in the January-February timeframe. The park web site will have information about this event: http://www.floridastateparks.org/forttaylor/default.cfm . There is a nominal fee to enter the state park.

Fort Jefferson. Also a fort occupied by Union forces throughout the war. Located in Dry Tortugas National Park, the fort is only accessible by boat or seaplane. Transport out to the fort is available from private vendors via a fee. The Park web site is: http://www.nps.gov/drto/index.htm

Gamble Plantation Historic State Park. The plantation home of Major Robert Gamble, who served in the Confederate Army during the war. The site is alleged to have provided a short-term refuge to Confederate Secretary of State Judah P. Benjamin as he fled the U.S. and there is a monument dedicated to Mr. Benjamin on the site. Web site: http://www.floridastateparks.org/gambleplantation/default.cfm . The park charges a nominal entrance fee.

Bibliography

Books and Reports

Anderson, Bern. *By Sea and by River. The Naval History of the Civil War.* Reprint by Da Capo Press. New York: Alfred A Knopf Inc., 1962.

Bearss, Edwin C. *Historic Structure Report, Fort Pickens, Historical Data Section, 1821-1895, Gulf Islands National Seashore, Florida/Mississippi.* Washington, D.C.: U.S. Department of the Interior, National Park Service, 1983.

Bennett, Michael J. *Union Jacks. Yankee Sailors in the Civil War.* Chapel Hill: University of North Carolina Press, 2004.

Browning, Robert M., Jr. *Success Is All That Was Expected. The South Atlantic Blockading Squadron during the Civil War.* Washington, D.C.: Brassey's Inc., 2002.

Buker, George E. *Blockaders, Refugees, & Contrabands. Civil War on Florida's Gulf Coast, 1861-1865.* Tuscaloosa: University of Alabama Press, 1993.

Campbell, R. Thomas. *Fire & Thunder. Exploits of the Confederate States Navy.* Shippensburg: Burd Street Press, 1997.

Canney, Donald L. *Lincoln's Navy. The Ships, Men and Organization, 1861-65.* London: Conway Maritime Press, 1998.

Chase, Susan F., and Carol S. Clark (editors). *Letters from the River War. Civil War on the St. Johns River 1862.* Jacksonville: National Park Service publication, 2007. Available at the gift shop at the Ft. Caroline National Monument.

First Presbyterian Church of Palatka. Records of the Minutes of the Session. Palatka, FL.

Hoehling, A. A. *Damn the Torpedoes! Naval Incidents of the Civil War.* Winston-Salem: John F. Blair Publisher, 1989.

Holland, Keith V., Lee B. Manley, and James W. Towart (editors). *The* Maple Leaf. *An Extraordinary American Civil War Shipwreck.* Jacksonville: St. Johns Archaeological Expeditions, Inc., 1993. (Available at the Mandarin Museum Gift Shop)

Hurley, Neil E. *Florida's Lighthouses in the Civil War.* Oakland Park: Middle River Press, 2007.

Koblas, John J. *The Swamp Fox & the* Columbine. St. Cloud: North Star Press, 2003.

Loderhose, Gary. *Way Down Upon the Suwannee River. Sketches of Florida During the Civil War.* San Jose: Authors Choice Press, 2000.

Macomber, Robert N. *At the Edge of Honor. A Novel of the Naval Civil War.* Sarasota: Pineapple Press, 2002.

Martin, Richard A., and Daniel L. Schafer. *Jacksonville's Ordeal by Fire. A Civil War History.* Jacksonville: Florida Publishing Co., 1984.

McPherson, James M. *War on the Waters. The Union and Confederate Navies, 1861-1865.* Chapel Hill: University of North Carolina Press, 2012.

Musicant, Ivan. *Divided Waters. The Naval History of the Civil War.* Edison: Castle Books (reprint of original HarperCollins Publishers edition), 2000.

Nulty, William H. *Confederate Florida. The Road to Olustee.* Tuscaloosa: University of Alabama Press, 1990.

Official Records of the Union and Confederate Navies in the War of Rebellion. 30 Volumes. Washington, D.C.: Government Printing Office, 1894-1922. NOTE: Main sources from this series were Volumes 12, 13, 15, 17 and 19.
http://digital.library.cornell.edu/m/moawar/ofre.html .

Pearce, George F. *Pensacola During the Civil War. A Thorn in the Side of the Confederacy.* Gainesville: University Press of Florida, 2000.

Ringle, Dennis J. *Life in Mr. Lincoln's Navy.* Annapolis: Naval Institute Press, 1998.

Schafer, Daniel L. *Thunder on the River. The Civil War in Northeast Florida.* Gainesville: University Press of Florida, 2010.

Simson, Jay W. *Naval Strategies of the Civil War. Confederate Innovations and Federal Opportunism.* Nashville: Cumberland House, 2001

Taylor, Paul. *Discovering the Civil War in Florida. A Reader and Guide.* Sarasota: Pineapple Press, 2001.

Taylor, Robert A. *Rebel Storehouse. Florida's Contribution to the Confederacy.* Tuscaloosa: University of Alabama Press, 2003.

Tucker, Spencer C. *Blue and Gray Navies. The Civil War Afloat.* Annapolis: Naval Institute Press, 2006.

Turner, Maxine. *Navy Gray. Engineering the Confederate Navy on the Chattahoochee and Apalachicola Rivers.* Macon: Mercer University Press, 1999 (re-issue of 1988 edition published by University of Alabama Press).

Wynne, Nick and Joe Crankshaw. *Florida Civil War Blockades. Battling for the Coast.* Charleston: The History Press, 2011.

Wynne, Lewis N. and Robert Taylor. *Florida In The Civil War.* Charleston: Arcadia Publishing, 2002.

Articles

Bearss, Edwin C. "Civil War Operations in and Around Pensacola. I. The Yankees Hold Fort Pickens in Defiance of the State of Florida." *Florida Historical Quarterly*, Vol. 36 (1957): 125-143.

Bearss, Edwin C. "Civil War Operations in and Around Pensacola. II. The Yankees Draw First Blood at Pensacola and the Battle of Santa Rosa Island." *Florida Historical Quarterly*, Vol. 36 (1957): 144-154.

Bearss, Edwin C. "Civil War Operations in and Around Pensacola. III. A Demonstration of the Superiority of the Federal Artillery." *Florida Historical Quarterly*, Vol. 36 (1957): 155-165.

Bearss, Edwin C. "Military Operations on the St. Johns, September-October 1862. Part I. The Union Navy Fails to Drive the Confederates From St. Johns Bluff." *Florida Historical Quarterly*, Vol. 42, No. 3 (1964): 232-247.

Bearss, Edwin C. "Military Operations on the St. Johns, September-October 1862. Part II. The Federals Capture St. Johns Bluff." *Florida Historical Quarterly,* Vol. 42, No. 4 (1964): 331-350.

Boyd, Mark F. "The Joint Operations of the Federal Army and Navy near St. Marks, Florida, March 1865." *Florida Historical Quarterly*, Vol. 29, No. 2 (1950): 96-124.

Buker, George E. "The Inner Blockade of Florida and the Wildcat Blockade-Runners." *North & South*, Vol. 4, No. 2 (2001): 70-85.

Cushman, Jr., Joseph D. "The Blockade and Fall of Apalachicola, 1861-1862." *Florida Historical Quarterly*, Vol. 41 (1962): 38-45.

Ekardt, David. "Fleet Marines of the American Civil War." *Civil War Historian,* Vol. 4, No. 5 (2008): 56-61.

Lonn, Ella. "The Extent and Importance of Federal Naval Raids on Salt-Making in Florida, 1862-1865." *Florida Historical Quarterly*, Vol. 10 (1932): 167-184.

Scofield, Walter K. "On Blockade Duty in Florida Waters. Excerpts from a Union Naval Officer's Diary." Edited by William J. Schellings. *Tequesta*, Vol. 15 (1955): 55-72

Strickland, Alice. "Blockade Runners." *Florida Historical Quarterly* Vol. 36 (1957): 85-93.

Web Resources

Civil War Navy Sesquicentennial. Official Blog Page. Brother Against Brother at Port Royal.

http://www.civilwarnavy150.blogspot.com/2011/11/brother-against-brother-at-port-royal.html.

Dictionary of American Naval Fighting Ships. Naval History and Heritage Command, http://www.history.navy.mil/danfs/index.html.

Dictionary of American Naval Fighting Ships. Confederate Forces Afloat. Naval History and Heritage Command, http://www.history.navy.mil/danfs/cfa-list.htm.

Dudley, William S. Going South: U.S. Navy Officer Resignations & Dismissals on the Eve of the Civil War. Naval History and Heritage Command, Washington, D.C., 1981.
http://www.history.navy.mil/library/online/going_south.htm .

Ekardt, David. The Navy's Great Salt Raids. Navy and Marine Living History Association "On-Deck!" web-zine, 2009.
http://www.navyandmarine.org/ondeck/1862saltraids.htm.

Ekardt, David. A Matter of Honor. The Seizure of the Pensacola Navy Yard. Navy and Marine Living History Association "On-Deck!" web-zine, 2005. http://www.navyandmarine.org/ondeck/1862Pensacola.htm.

Ekardt, David. Orderly Sergeant Christopher Nugent. Medal of Honor Winner at Crystal River, Florida. Navy and Marine Living History Association "On-Deck!" web-zine, undated.
http://www.navyandmarine.org/ondeck/1862USMC_MoH.htm .

Florida Department of State. Needs More Salt. Florida Memory Project blog post. July 25, 2012.
http://floridamemory.com/blog/2012/07/25/needs-more-salt/.

Howard, Frank. Wakulla County Florida. Some Civil War Action. 1993. www.littletownmart.com/fdh/st-marks_civil_war.htm.

John Milton (Florida politician). Wikipedia:
http://en.wikipedia.org/wiki/John_Milton_(Florida_politician) .

Maple Leaf Shipwreck. An Extraordinary American Civil War Shipwreck. http://www.mapleleafshipwreck.com/index.htm .

National Park Service. The River War: The Timucuan Preserve in the Civil War.
http://www.nps.gov/timu/planyourvisit/upload/civil_war_site_bulletin.pdf .

Naval History and Heritage Command. Officers of the Continental and U.S. Navy and Marine Corps, 1775-1900.
http://www.history.navy.mil/books/callahan/index.htm.

Port Columbus National Civil War Naval Museum. Exhibits, CSS Chattahoochee. http://portcolumbus.org/exhibits

The Marine Corps Gazette. Marines in the American Civil War.
https://www.mca-marines.org/gazette/photogallery/marines-american-civil-war.

Zerfas, Lew. Naval Action reports for Tampa Bay. USS Fort Henry Living History Association .
http://www.ussforthenry.com/USSFHpdf/Navy_Action_Tampa_Bay.PDF

Index

African Americans in the U.S. Navy, 17
Ammen, Daniel, 39
Anclote River, Brooksville Raid, 128
Atlantic Blockading Squadron, 6
Apalachicola, 60
    importance as a cotton port, 60
Apalachicola Bay
    cutting out of schooner *Finland*, 61
    Lt. Gift's raid in, 68
Apalachicola River, 60
    destruction of CSS *Chattahoochee* on, 67
    1865 raid from USS *Midnight* on, 146
Bailey, Theodorus, 9, 65
Baxter, I.B., 40, 110, 117
Bayport, Union Navy raids on, 129, 132
Blockade Board, 6
Blockade runners, 5
    Florida as a destination, 25
Browne, William R., 40
    commanding salt works raids, 57
Buchanan, Franklin, 11
Cedar Keys, 133
    ambush of U.S. Navy landing party, 134
    first Union Navy raid at, 133
Charlotte Harbor
    attack on Union landing party supporting Unionist rangers, 119
    cutting out expeditions in, 116, 117
    formation of the Refugee Rangers, 118
    Union Navy blockade efforts, 114
Crane, Henry, assistance to the Union, 110
Crissey, Edwin, 40, 57
C.S. Navy
    African Americans in, 17
    officers in, 14
    presence in Florida, 24
    speculation on how they could have contributed in Florida, 159
C.S. Navy Cruisers (raiders), 22
    CSS *Alabama*, 12, 22
    CSS *Florida*, 22
    CSS *Shenandoah*, 22
    CSS *Sumter*, 22
CS *Darlington*, 76
CS *Jefferson Davis*, 23
CS *Gov. Milton*, 106

CS *Hattie*, 26, 107
CS *Kate Dale*, 124
CS *Scottish Chief*, 124
CS *Sumter*, 107
CSS *Chattahoochee*
    boiler explosion, 67
CSS *Jackson*, 159
CSS *Spray*, 71
CSS *Stonewall*, 152
Dahlgren, John A., 7
Drayton, Percival, 35, 40, 74
Du Pont, Samuel F., 8
East Gulf Blockading Squadron, 9
Egmont Key, 31
    establishment of secondary Union Navy base, 121
English, Earl, 41, 104, 134
Farragut, David G., 9
    appointed first USN Vice Admiral, 10
Fernandina, 74
Fox, Gustavus V., 1
Ft. Brooke, 28
    Confederate takeover of, 28
    Union bombardments of, 122
    Union occupation of, 127
Ft. Clinch, 27
    Union retaking of, 74
Ft. Jefferson, 34
Ft. Marion, 27
Ft. Pickens, 31
    reinforcement of garrison, 32
    Confederate assault on, 49
    artillery duel, 49
Ft. Zachary Taylor, 34
Gamble Mansion, Manatee County, 157
Gift, George, 44, 65
Gulf Blockading Squadron, 6
Guthrie, John J., 44, 66
Harmony, David B., 41, 73
Hillsborough River, Union raid up the river, 124
Howell, John C., 41, 69, 134
Indian River Lagoon, 109
    efforts to close down, 109
    Henry Crane's actions in, 110
Jacksonville,
    first Union occupation of, 78
Jones, Catesby ap Roger, 44

Jupiter Inlet, 109
Key West, 34
Lighthouses, Florida, 29
McCauley, Edward Y., 41, 128, 132
McGary, Charles P., 45, 140
McLaughlin, Augustus, 45
Mallory, Stephen R., 3
    naval strategy, 4
    arrest at the end of the war, 148
    final resting place in Pensacola, 150
Marines, U.S. and C.S., 21
Mayport Mills Navy Base, 78
Mervine, William, 6, 47
Mosquito Inlet, 100
    ambush of Union Navy landing party, 102
    Union Navy attack on New Smyrna, 105
    destruction of schooner *Florence Nightingale*, 104
Mosquito Lagoon, 100
New Smyrna, 100
North Atlantic Blockading Squadron, 6
Nugent, Sgt. Christopher, medal of honor recipient, 131-32
Ochlockonee River, 71
    cutting out of schooner *Caroline Gertrude*, 72
Palatka, 79
    first encounter with Union forces, 79
Pensacola Bay
    burning of dry dock by Union, 47
    Union raid and destruction of the CS *Judah*, 48
Pensacola Navy Yard, 31
    Confederate takeover, 31
    Confederate evacuation, 51
River warfare, 35
Rogers, C.R.P., 42, 76, 81
St. Andrews Bay, 53
St. Augustine
   Union re-occupation of, 81
St. Johns Bluff
    construction of earthworks, 83
    first gunboat engagement, 84
    second gunboat engagement, 85
    taking of the battery on, 88
St. Johns River
    ambush of the *Columbine* by J.J. Dickison, 98
    ambush of Union landing party at Magnolia Springs, 92
    capture of a landing party from USS *Ottawa*, 145
    cutting out expeditions on the southern river, 106

        interactions with civilians, slaves and southerners, 81
        patrols in 1862, 90
        patrols in 1863, 93
        sinking of Union transports by rebel torpedoes, 94-6
St. Marks River, 68
        Union invasion ("Battle of Natural Bridge"), 148
Sailors, U.S. Navy
        grog ration, 19
        mess, 17
        non-commissioned officers, 16
        pay rates, 15
        prize money, 16
        skills, 16
        serving on watches, 20
Salt works, 53
        raids on Big Bend coast, 134, 140, 142
        raids on St. Andrews Bay, 54-60
        raids on Tampa Bay, 126
        salt, importance of, 52
Sarasota Bay, 119
Schooner yacht *America*, 80
Seahorse Key, 30
        establishment of secondary Union Navy base, 134
Semmes, Raphael, 12, 30
South Atlantic Blockading Squadron, 7
Steedman, Charles, 38, 42, 85
Stevens, Thomas H., 42, 78, 79
Suwannee River, capture of blockade runners, 137-38, 155
Tampa, 28
Tampa Bay
        Union raids in, 122
Tattnall, Josiah, 13
Torpedoes, Confederate use on the St. Johns River, 94
US Steamer *Maple Leaf*, 95
U.S. Navy
        conversion of merchant steamers, 2
        death of sailors in the Civil War, 161
        number of men at the end of the war, 3
        number of ships at war's outbreak, 1
        officers in, 14
        organizing civilian/slave resistance, 35, 158
        overall role in the Civil War, 157
        presence in Florida, 24
        role in the War in Florida, 157
USS *Adela*, 124
USS *Albatross*, 54

USS *Annie*, 141
    destruction of, 150
USS *Beauregard*, 105, 114, 124
USS *Bienville*, 38
USS *Brooklyn*, 6, 32, 47
USS *Cimarron*, 85, 90
USS *Colorado*, 47
USS *Fort Henry*, 128, 135
USS *Fox*, 142
USS *Gem of the Sea*, 110, 117
USS *Hatteras*, 133
USS *Henry Andrew*, 102
USS *Keystone State*, 101
USS *Kingfisher*, 53, 138
    ambush of watering party on the Aucilla River, 139-40
    St. Joseph Bay salt works raid, 53
USS *Midnight*, 146
  raid on the Apalachicola River, 147
USS *Mohawk*, 69
USS *Montgomery*, 37, 60
USS *Niagara*, 6, 49
USS *Nita*, 138
USS *Ottawa*, 78
    chase of a rebel train, 75
    expedition to Palatka, 79
USS *Patroon*, 83, 85
USS *Paul Jones*, 85
USS *Penguin*, 102
USS *Pursuit*, 124
USS *R. R. Cuyler*, 38, 61
USS *Restless*, 57, 116
USS *Rosalie*, 116
USS *Sabine*, 32, 47
USS *Sagamore*, 104, 122, 128
USS *Somerset*
    in Apalachicola Bay, 67
    off St. Marks River, 69
    salt works raid at Seahorse Key, 134
USS *St. Louis*, 32, 47
USS *Stars and Stripes*, 70-72
USS *Tahoma*
    actions at Cedar Key, 134
    raid on St. Marks/Goose Creek salt works, 73
    actions in Tampa Bay, 124
    raid on Taylor County salt works, 140
USS *Uncas*, 83

USS *Wabash*, 8, 81, 103
USS *Water Witch*, 87, 90
USS *Wyandotte*, 31
   in the defense of Ft. Pickens, 46
Waccasassa River, 131
       ambush of U.S. Navy landing party, 135
Weeks, Edmund C., 43
Welles, Gideon, 1
West Gulf Blockading Squadron, 9
Woodhull, Maxwell, 43, 87, 91
Yellow Bluff, earthworks, 83

www.ingramcontent.com/pod-product-compliance
Lightning Source LLC
Chambersburg PA
CBHW071917290426
44110CB00013B/1383